Even More
SIGNS OF OUR TIMES

More Biblical Reasons Why This Could Be the Generation of the Rapture

MICHAEL SAWDY

**BIBLICAL SIGNS
PUBLISHING**

Published in Plymouth, Michigan, by Biblical Signs Publishing, an imprint of BiblicalSigns.com.

This Book may be purchased in bulk for educational, business, fund-raising, or sales promotional use. For information, please email BiblicalSigns@gmail.com.

Unless otherwise noted, Scripture quotations in this book are taken from the King James or English Standard Versions. Public domain.

All italics in Scripture quotations were added by the author for emphasis.

ISBN 9780578452395

Library of Congress Control Number: 2019901844

Cover Design by MichaEL Sawdy.

Printed in the United States of America

Even More
SIGNS OF OUR TIMES

TO LORD JESUS:
Thank You for every blessing that I have ever received from the Father in this life through You. I especially give You thanks for my parents, brother, Jacob, and entire family. Thank You for Your Heavenly gifts of grace, mercy, wisdom, and salvation. Thank You, above all, for Your Holy Spirit and Word - which guide me daily on the right path. Thank You for using me to spread the good news of Your return to all nations of the world. I'm forever humbled and grateful for all that You do in me and through me. Glory to You and to our Father in Heaven always my Lord. I love You forever.

CONTENTS

INTRODUCTION

THE RAPTURE

FOR THE LORD HIMSELF SHALL DESCEND FROM HEAVEN
WITH A SHOUT, WITH THE VOICE OF THE ARCHANGEL, AND
WITH THE TRUMP OF GOD: AND THE DEAD IN CHRIST SHALL
RISE FIRST: THEN WE WHICH ARE ALIVE AND REMAIN SHALL
BE CAUGHT UP TOGETHER WITH THEM IN THE CLOUDS, TO
MEET THE LORD IN THE AIR: AND SO SHALL WE EVER BE WITH
THE LORD. COMFORT ONE ANOTHER WITH THESE WORDS.

- 1ST THESSALONIANS 4:16-18

COMFORT... THAT IS WHAT hope in the long-awaited Rapture of the faithful is meant to bring. How can we instill that hope in those around us, so that we may truly *comfort* one another, in a generation plagued by despair, evil, hatred, and violence? Exactly as Saint Paul told us to... *"with these words."* With the words that describe our Lord's descent from Heaven to rescue us from this wicked world, both the dead and living of His Church, before all hell breaks loose on Planet Earth. This message brings a believer lasting peace and serenity in an ever troubled world that is filled with chaos. It reminds us - in the midst of rampant evil - that the worse things get, the closer we draw to that glorious day.

That day when our corruptible mortal bodies are transformed into incorruptible immortal bodies, and when we'll finally get to see our Lord face to face. How could anyone not be comforted with that thought? Unfortunately, today, there appears to be a lot of believers who do not ascribe to the doctrine of the Rapture - who believe we will endure every plague and judgment foretold in the Book of Revelation. They obviously don't know the God of the Book they claim to believe. Our LORD is a just, faithful, and merciful God. He delights in the righteous, and He rewards those who diligently heed His Word and seek His Face.

When He first destroyed the wicked from off the face of the earth in the Flood of Noah's days, notice how He preserved Noah and his family on the Ark - keeping them *out of* global judgment. Remember the two words "out of" going forward, because they're key to understanding the Rapture. Noah did not endure the wrath of God along with the wicked. Also, think back to the judgment of Sodom and Gomorrah, and how the LORD delivered Lot and his family *out of* it for Abraham's sake. Lot did not endure God's punishment along with the wicked.

So, why then are there some believers who think that we will be going through the worst tribulation the world has ever seen - along with the wicked? It doesn't make sense that God would all of a sudden change the way that He deals with the righteous and the wicked. His Word is clear that He's the same yesterday, today, and forever (Hebrews 13:8). He tells us that He will never change (Malachi 3:6). The advocates of a Post-Tribulation Rapture have obviously never read the words of Lord Jesus in Revelation...

"BECAUSE YOU HAVE KEPT THE WORD OF MY PATIENCE, I ALSO WILL KEEP YOU FROM THE HOUR OF TEMPTATION, WHICH SHALL COME UPON ALL THE WORLD, TO TRY THEM THAT DWELL UPON THE EARTH." - REVELATION 3:10

I said to remember the words "out of," because (in English translations of the Holy Bible) we read "keep you *from* the hour" in that verse of Revelation. The word "from" in the Greek is "ek," which means "*out of*." So, contrary to the thinking of my brothers and sisters who expect to go through the seven-year Tribulation, Jesus didn't mince words when promising that He would keep us *out of* it altogether. Instead of us boarding an Ark like Noah, or fleeing to another place like Lot, the Lord Himself comes down to evacuate us from Earth before God's judgments are poured out. I don't understand how some Christians can read their Bibles from front to back, and believe the LORD would somehow allow us to endure the worst tribulation in human history. He will not.

Besides Christians who think that we'll be going through the Tribulation, there is also a group of so-called believers who mock the idea of the Rapture and Christ's imminent return altogether. This group believes we shouldn't be concerned about the Rapture or Jesus' return at all, because they say every generation before us believed that they would experience these events and did not. Oh, how I wish that this backslidden group of Christians would read my previous book. In it, I give many irrefutable reasons why our generation is the *first* in world history to see specific prophecies related to the Lord's return being fulfilled.

I explained why no generation before 1948 could have had any hope of seeing Christ return, because there had to be a Nation of Israel on Earth for the "Last Days" signs of the Bible to mean anything. Until the spring of '48, there was no Israel on the map. There hadn't been for thousands of years. If you haven't yet, read *The Signs of Our Times*. I go into great detail as to why a reborn Israel is central to Jesus' Second Coming. Don't listen to Rapture scoffers. They're too comfortable in this sinful world. Thus, they don't want to see our Lord return in this day and age. They are actually *fulfilling* a "Last Days" sign...

"THERE SHALL COME IN THE LAST DAYS SCOFFERS, WALKING AFTER THEIR OWN LUSTS, AND SAYING, WHERE IS THE PROMISE OF HIS COMING? FOR SINCE THE FATHERS FELL ASLEEP, ALL THINGS CONTINUE AS THEY WERE FROM THE BEGINNING OF THE CREATION." - 2ND PETER 3:3-4

There are also Christians believing that a Rapture of Christ's Church already occurred, that Jesus has already returned to Earth (spiritually - not physically), and that the Book of Revelation has already been fulfilled. None of these beliefs make one bit of sense whatsoever. Christians believing these things, known as Preterists, have obviously never studied Biblical Prophecy.

First off, millions of believers would go missing all over this world simultaneously during the Rapture. When in world history has that ever happened? The answer is *never*. Second, the Bible is clear that Jesus' Second Coming - like His First Coming - would be in the flesh, and that *every eye* would see Him (Revelation 1:7 - Zechariah 14:4 - Matthew 16:27, 24:30 and 25:31 - Mark 13:26 - Luke 21:27 - Acts 1:11 - John 14:3). It will not be an invisible "spiritual" return. If it were to be, God would have told us so. He did not. Instead, He was clear that Christ's *literal* feet will hit the *literal* Mount of Olives in Jerusalem upon His return to the earth. Read all of the Biblical verses that I listed above, and you'll find there can be no logical argument for an *invisible* return to Earth.

Finally, I cannot understand how anyone ascribes to the view that Revelation has already been fulfilled. That's nonsense. When in history has 1/3 of Earth and 1/3 of mankind been destroyed? When have all men and women of the earth ever worshipped the AntiChrist, as he sat in Jerusalem's Temple declaring himself to be God? When did the inhabitants of Earth ever receive the Mark of the Beast in their right hands or foreheads, in order to buy and sell goods? When did all nations of the world come against Israel in an attempt to destroy the Jewish State? When did Christ and His Armies come down to save Israel from certain destruction? When did the Jews of the world look upon Jesus and realize that He was truly their Messiah all along?

When was Satan cast into the bottomless pit? When did "New Jerusalem" descend from Heaven? When was Christ's Kingdom ever set up on Earth, and when did believers of the world rule and reign with Him from the Holy Land of Israel? Can anyone, who believes the nonsensical theory that the Book of Revelation has already been fulfilled, point to a time in history when those events have occurred? Obviously, you cannot - because those prophecies have never been fulfilled! The groups of backslidden Christians that I've addressed are ignoring the numerous "Last Days" signs occurring all around them. Whether due to fear of prophesied End Times events taking place, or due to living unrepentant lives, they do not want to witness our Lord return anytime soon.

They are of the crowd in today's Church that love to quote Matthew 24:36, in which Jesus said, "Of that day and hour knows no man, no, not the angels of Heaven, but My Father only." They use this verse as an excuse to not be looking for, or recognizing, the Latter-Day signs happening all around us. This is dangerous for a Christian to do. Yes, Jesus said that we would not know the "day or hour," but He also taught that we *would know* the season. Back up just a few verses in Chapter 24 - to verse 33 - and notice how Jesus said, "When you shall see all these things, *know that I Am near*, even at the doors."

He also said, in the Book of Luke, "When these things begin to come to pass, then look up, and lift up your heads; for your redemption draweth near... So likewise you, when you see these things come to pass, *know you* that the Kingdom of God is near at hand" (Luke 21:28-31). What *things* was He referring to exactly? The *signs* of His return. If we are not to be concerned with His return, because "no one" knows the day or hour, then why'd He ever bother giving us signs to watch for in the first place?

The reason why He said no one would know the exact day or hour of His return is because days and hours differ all around the globe. 2:00 am in Israel is 7:00 pm in the northeastern U.S., 6:00 pm in parts of the southern U.S., 4:00 pm in the western U.S., and 12 noon in Britain. Due to different time zones across the world, days and hours can never be the same. So, there is no way anyone could ever predict the exact date and time of the Second Coming. They would have to give multiple days and hours in order to fit their prediction into every time zone. That is why Lord Jesus has commanded us to be ready at *all times*, especially when the signs that He gave begin to occur - and they have undoubtedly begun.

This is why I believe the Spirit called me to write these books - because the time of our redemption draweth near, and sleeping Christians need a *wake-up call*. I pray that my books will sound an alarm in the hearts, souls, and minds of all believers. It is high time to awake out of sleep, to give heed unto the Word of God, to listen attentively to His Holy Spirit, and to look up, because the King is coming! Our King is coming! ARE YOU READY?

BEHOLD, I SHEW YOU A MYSTERY; WE SHALL NOT ALL SLEEP, BUT WE SHALL ALL BE CHANGED, IN A MOMENT, IN THE TWINKLING OF AN EYE, AT THE LAST TRUMP: FOR THE TRUMPET SHALL SOUND, AND THE DEAD SHALL BE RAISED INCORRUPTIBLE, AND WE SHALL BE CHANGED.

- 1ST CORINTHIANS 15:51-52

CHAPTER ONE

THE SIGNS OF OUR TIMES CONTINUE

AS HE SAT UPON THE MOUNT OF OLIVES, THE DISCIPLES
CAME UNTO JESUS PRIVATELY, SAYING, TELL US, WHEN SHALL
THESE THINGS BE? AND WHAT SHALL BE THE SIGN OF THY
COMING, AND OF THE END OF THE AGE?

- MATTHEW 24:3

IN MY FIRST BOOK, *The Signs of Our Times*, I covered twelve specific Latter-Day signs that could be heralding the Rapture in our generation. This Sequel picks up where that book had left off, covering *Even More* Signs occurring in our lifetimes. But before I delve into them, there've been many new developments regarding the signs that I previously addressed. Therefore, in these first few chapters, I am going to revisit them...

ANTI-SEMITISM

The Anti-Defamation League (ADL) reported that the number of anti-Semitic incidents in the United States was nearly 60% higher in 2017 than in 2016, which was the largest single-year increase on record. A 2018 EU (European Union) poll found that 90% of Europe's Jews felt anti-Semitism increased exponentially over the previous five years. Also last year, France saw a 75% increase in anti-Semitic crimes; and there had been a 60% rise in Canada. In October 2018, the worst anti-Semitic attack in American history occurred. A demonic psychopath carried out the deadliest attack ever on U.S. Jews, opening fire on the congregation of the Tree of Life Synagogue in Pennsylvania, murdering 11.

Since the shooter was an unrepentant Jew-hater, I refuse to even mention his name. Anti-Semites are of the devil, and their names should be erased from history - never to be remembered. The only time that I ever name anti-Semites in my books, or on my website, is when I expose or warn against those in positions of power and influence. That is exactly what Harvard Law School professor emeritus, Alan Dershowitz, has been doing. Though he has been a lifelong Democrat, he recently chastised his party for turning a "blind eye" to the alarming rise of anti-Semitism within its ranks. He points specifically to the growing anti-Israel animus of the far-left, especially regarding support for the BDS (Boycott, Divestment, and Sanctions) movement.

The new breed of Dems that Dershowitz has alluded to are namely Muslim Congresswomen Ilhan Omar of Minnesota and Rashida Tlaib of Michigan, the Muslim DNC Deputy Chairman Keith Ellison, and Muslim leader of the Women's March, Linda Sarsour. Dershowitz, himself, doesn't hold a personal bias against Muslims; but there is no denying that the religion of Islam teaches a bitter hatred of the Jews and Israel. I go into great detail about Islamic disdain for God's Chosen people in my previous book.

Dershowitz rightly accuses Dems of tolerating anti-Semitism. He has said, "The Democratic Party, in itself, isn't anti-Semitic, but they are tolerating anti-Semitism on the hard-left part of their base because they don't want to alienate their base. Keith Ellison gets elected Deputy Chairman of the Democratic National Party, and he had close associations with Louis Farrakhan and falsely denied them." For those not familiar, Farrakhan is the Nation of Islam leader who has called the Jews "Satanic" and "termites."

Dershowitz says many members of the Congressional Black Caucus have had associations with Louis Farrakhan. Even former President Obama had closely allied himself with the self-avowed Jew-hater. Dershowitz (a Jewish man) said of a Obama-Farrakhan photo from 2005, that was suppressed by the mainstream media, "If I had known that the President posed, smiling with Farrakhan, when he was a Senator, I wouldn't have campaigned for Obama." Being friends with a man like Farrakhan may explain the former President's hostility toward Israel.

While both parties today - Republican and Democrat - have problems with anti-Semites, from the alt-right and hard-left, it is clear that only one of the two parties is propping them up unto positions of power. Dershowitz says the Republican Party does a better job in condemning anti-Semites on the alt-right, and that the Democrats must do a better job of condemning anti-Semites on the hard-left. Dershowitz is very concerned about the future of Jews, and their treatment, in the Democrat Party. With Jew-haters like Omar, Tlaib, and Sarsour being poster children for the party, he has good reason for his concern. All three women promote the BDS campaign, which publicly calls for the destruction of Israel.

Sarsour has proudly admitted that her family in Palestine has committed terror attacks against the Israelis, and also refuses to condemn them or to apologize for it. Her husband has expressed support for Palestinian terror group Hamas, while Linda has held events raising money for them and the Muslim Brotherhood. She advocates strongly for Sharia Law, while claiming to be a "liberal feminist." If that is not an oxymoron, then I don't know what is! The Democrats need to do some serious soul-searching, or else they will come to find that many souls in their party have already been sold; and I'll give you one guess who the buyer is. Here is a hint: His name starts with an "S," and ends with "ATAN."

CHRISTIAN PERSECUTION

Believers are still facing extreme persecution all across the world. The current Top 10 worst offenders are North Korea, Afghanistan, Somalia, Libya, Pakistan, Sudan, Eritrea, Yemen, Iran, and India. The deadliest country for followers of Christ, in 2018, has been the African nation of Nigeria - where it's been reported that over 6,000 Christians were murdered for their faith in just the first half of the year alone. The Christian Association of Nigeria warns that "Christianity is on the brink of extinction" there, due to the rapid spread of Islamic ideology in the country.

A report released in late 2018 by Aid to the Church in Need (ACN), on "Religious Freedom in the World," revealed that half a billion Christians today face persecution across the globe. ACN reports that Religious Freedom is declining in 1 out of 5 nations of the world. Outside of North Korea, India and Islamic nations (which account for 8 of the top 10), China is becoming one of the most dangerous places on Earth for Christians to live. In 2018, a prominent Religious Freedom activist from China, Reverend Bob Fu, had told the U.S. Congress that the Chinese government was preparing a 5-year plan to conform Christianity to Socialism. He said that their intent was to essentially "rewrite the Holy Bible."

Under the leadership of Communist President, Xi Jinping, the Chinese government regularly arrests Christians, destroys Crosses (well over 10,000), raids and closes churches, and they even *burn* Bibles. The government forces many Christians in the country to sign papers renouncing their faith.

Here in the United States, even though the Supreme Court is becoming more conservative and friendly toward Bible believers, anti-Christian liberals continue to take believers to trial before the highest court in the land. They are targeting Christians who refuse to bow to their Godless agenda. Case in point, after he had won his SCOTUS case, upholding his right to refuse baking cakes for gay weddings, Colorado baker Jack Phillips is being sued *again*. This time around, because he objected to make a cake celebrating transgenderism. The Court had previously ruled 7-2 in his favor, arguing that - as a Christian - he was targeted by Colorado's Civil Rights Commission due to his beliefs. Apparently, the liberals in Colorado did not get the Supreme Court's memo.

Just a few weeks after the SCOTUS decision, the State ruled Phillips "violated the law by refusing to make a cake celebrating a gender transition." In 2017, a transgender lawyer asked Phillips to make the "transition celebration" cake. When he had declined on religious grounds, he was swiftly sued. It is important to note that Jack had also turned down requests to make cakes celebrating the devil, drugs, witchcraft, and sexually explicit images. So, contrary to what the lamestream media says, he doesn't single out anyone for discrimination. He opposes celebrating *anything* that the Bible has dubbed sinful. It's also telling that many of the cake requests I mentioned had come from the *same* lawyer who is suing Phillips.

Many believers across this country have come under attack by the lunatic left for not embracing the transgender revolution that's been sweeping across America. Last year, Nicholas Meriwether, a professor at an Ohio college, was punished by his university for refusing to refer to a transgender student by their preferred gender pronoun. Meriwether, an Evangelical Christian who is a 22-year employee of Shawnee State University, answered a male student's question with "Yes, sir." His response was directed to a biological male who now *identifies* as female. The student, Alena Bruening, approached Meriwether after class and demanded that he refer to him using only feminine pronouns. Meriwether refused.

Bruening then promised to get him fired and used derogatory language toward him. Meriwether says he has always referred to every student as either sir, ma'am, mister, or miss. Due to SSU's anti-Christian "non-discrimination policy," the acting Dean of the college charged Meriwether with causing "a hostile environment" in his classroom for refusing to violate his beliefs. The professor submitted a grievance request to his union, arguing that SSU had violated his freedom of expression. When he met with a school administrator and a union representative to explain how he felt his Religious Freedom was being attacked, he says that they "openly laughed" at his convictions and denied his grievance request.

In October of 2018, anti-Christian posters started popping up near trash cans across New York City. The posters featured two images - a white man wearing a "Make America Great Again" hat, holding a Chick-Fil-A cup; and a white woman, also wearing a "MAGA" hat, holding a Bible. The posters messages' had read: "Keep NYC trash-free."

Hatred of President Donald Trump is nothing new, and we all know how dirty politics can get. So, attacks against his "MAGA" slogan and his supporters are not surprising. What is surprising, and deeply disturbing, is that Christians are dubbed as "trash" in NYC. Worse, the lamestream media barely reported it. I am sure that if someone made similar posters featuring Muslims, instead of Christians, it would have been around-the-clock headline news.

TERRORISM

Islamic terrorism is still the greatest threat to Christians globally. Suicide attacks in churches, schools, hotels, and markets continue to claim the lives of hundreds of believers at a time. Due to great progress that's been made by the Trump administration in its war on ISIS, terrorists have been brainstorming new methods to harm American citizens. In the upcoming chapters on "Pestilences" and "Wars and Rumours of Wars," you'll learn why bioterrorism and power-grid attacks are at the top of their list.

THE ENEMIES OF ISRAEL

Recent clashes between Israel and Hamas terrorists in Gaza have Middle East experts believing another war, like the battle of 2014, is ever on the horizon. In that war, Hamas fired over 4,000 rockets into the Jewish State. In July of 2017, the Palestinian terror group launched nearly 200 rockets into Israeli communities in *one day*. A month later, they fired another 220. In the fall of 2018, Hamas bombarded Israel with 300+ rockets - in less than 5 hours. In the spring of 2019, Hamas and Islamic Jihad terrorists fired *over 700 rockets* into southern Israel. Another war is inevitable.

SIGNS IN THE HEAVENS

In 2013, an asteroid entered Earth's atmosphere over Russia as a fireball and exploded above the city of Chelyabinsk. Over 7,000 buildings, across six cities, were damaged due to the shock wave from the explosion. About 1,500 people were injured. It had been the largest recorded object to encounter Earth in over a century. In 2018, another meteor struck the earth - actually exploding in my local area of Michigan. It sparked a small earthquake in the Metro Detroit area. I actually witnessed the jaw-dropping event, as I saw a huge burst of light in my backyard around 8:00 pm. After hours of trying to figure out what I had seen, the local news confirmed a meteorite had fallen nearby. I believe these events were a preview of Revelation 6:13, when "the stars of heaven fall unto the earth."

Another rare event, in 2018, had occurred a few weeks after the publication of my first book; and that was the "longest Blood Moon of the 21st Century." A Total Lunar Eclipse of such length won't appear in the skies again until 2123. I think it is safe to say that we will not be around for the next one!

EARTHQUAKES

Indonesia was rocked by a massive 7.5 magnitude earthquake in late 2018, and a devastating tsunami followed. Just over a month later, both the ground and residents of Alaska were rattled by a powerful 7.0 earthquake. The major temblor had violently shook buildings, damaged roads, and knocked out power in Anchorage - Alaska's most populated city. The quake was felt up to 400 miles outside of the city. There were several reports of serious damage. Walls had been cracked, ceiling tiles fell, contents of store shelves were littered across floors, and an onramp to a freeway collapsed. One resident of Palmer, Alaska, said that it was "the most violent earthquake" she ever experienced in her 37 years as a resident.

At least four airports closed in the State following the quake, and Alaska's Governor issued a disaster declaration. Nearly 2,000 aftershocks shook the region within three days. Jesus prophesied that, in the *Last Days* leading up to His imminent return, there'd be "powerful earthquakes" around the world. In my first book, I explained that quakes over 7.0 magnitude are dubbed "powerful." Since the year 2000, there've been about 300 earthquakes that fall into this category. That's an average of over 15 per year. I believe the Alaska quake may have been a forerunner for more powerful earthquakes coming to the USA in the very near future.

EXTREME WEATHER

The 2018 Hurricane season was officially the most active season ever recorded, and the most memorable name of that season was my namesake - MICHAEL. In *The Signs of Our Times*, I had told readers to keep an eye on the upcoming Biblically-named storms - especially Michael. As I predicted, the historic storm that bore the name of God's most powerful Archangel was added to the list of retired hurricanes bearing Biblical names. Catching forecasters off guard, by quickly strengthening to a Category 4 within just 3 days, Michael made landfall in the Florida Panhandle as the most powerful hurricane on record to ever strike that area of the Gulf Coast. Packing 155 mph winds, and up to 175 mph gusts, it was the first Category 5 to strike Florida in almost 3 decades!

There had been States of Emergency declared in the Sunshine State, Georgia, and Alabama. About 3-million people were under evacuation orders, and around 3.7-million were under hurricane watches or warnings as Michael approached. The storm had made landfall in Mexico Beach, Florida, and absolutely destroyed that oceanside city. The hurricane also devastated Panama City Beach. Michael remained a hurricane for twelve hours after its landfall. Describing the damage, a Florida police officer said that it looked *"like the Apocalypse."*

In the "Extreme Weather" chapter of my previous book, I had documented connections between many Biblically-named storms and America's mistreatment of Israel. While not all such storms in our nation's history were associated with the U.S. doing Israel wrong, there can be no question that a majority were. This time around, I don't believe that Michael was connected to U.S.-Israeli relations. I couldn't find American leadership doing anything that could be considered anti-Israel during Michael's life cycle. But I still firmly believe it was a judgment sent by the LORD upon this backslidden nation. As I stated in my previous book, America has given Him far too many reasons to pour out His Wrath upon this rebellious people.

Besides mistreatment of His beloved Israel, there are at least seven national abominations that I can think of which provoke the LORD to anger. They are...

1. Removing Him from the public square
2. National decline in Biblical belief
3. Widespread blasphemy and moral decay
4. False god worship
5. Legalizing SIN – such as same-sex marriage
6. Sexual rebellion against God
7. Holocaust of America's babies through abortion

Going down this list, do you think that our nation is deserving of God's judgments? I think America is more than deserving. If it weren't for His merciful and patient nature, the USA would have been wiped out a long time ago - especially under the previous President's administration. So, if it was not connected to Israel, was Hurricane Michael connected to any of the abominations that I listed above? I think it was. Michael formed in the Caribbean as Tropical Depression #14 on October 6th. In my research, I had discovered that a God-provoking SCOTUS decision occurred on the *exact same date*.

On October 6th, 2014, Barack Obama's left-leaning Supreme Court paved the way for nationwide legalization of Gay Marriage (coming 9 months later, in June 2015). Exactly 4 years *to the day* of Michael's formation, the Court declined to hear appeals from States seeking to uphold bans on same-sex marriage. The Court slamming the door on those cases, and all future appeals, cleared the way for Gay Marriage to expand to well over 30 states and, ultimately, all 50 states by the next year. Michael forming on the anniversary of that 2014 decision and also being the **14**th Tropical Depression was no coincidence.

Archangel Michael is God's Warrior who fights against evil. He makes war on anything that is against our God. The Bible tells us that he was the one who battled Lucifer (the devil) and sent him falling from Heaven. Thus, it is fitting that the judgment for a history-changing wicked decision - by what was a Supreme Court majority under the influence of Satan - bore the name of God's Angel who wars against all that is evil.

In my previous book, I also wrote about how God destroyed the theory of "man-made" global warming when he had brought a historically cold winter in 2017-2018. He did it again, and then some, at the close of the 2018-2019 season. In late January, tens of millions of Americans experienced unbearable temperatures of 30 degrees below zero (or lower) during the "Polar Vortex." Some areas within the northern U.S. saw temps fall as low as 60 degrees below zero! In my area of southeast Michigan, the freezing temps had the ability to cause frostbite within 5-10 minutes throughout a 48-hour period. Also in the Metro-Detroit area, 99-year-old low temperature records were shattered.

In nearby Illinois, Chicago broke records as well - registering temps nearly 50 degrees below zero with the windchill; and a new record low temperature for the State of Illinois was set during the Vortex. Alabama, Illinois, Michigan, Mississippi, and Wisconsin all declared States of Emergency. Illinois and Wisconsin had been among 6 States that recorded temps as low as the South Pole. The other 4 were North Dakota, South Dakota, Minnesota, and Iowa. Speaking of Minnesota and Iowa, Minneapolis had recorded 14 consecutive hours of "Real Feel" temps of 50 degrees below zero; and in Des Moines, Iowa, the temperature fell to nearly 60 below!

Sometimes I really wish the "global warming" theorists were right, because the record-breaking cold's absolutely miserable for those of us who live in the North. I believe the Polar Vortex was meant to be miserable for the Northeast, especially for New York, being a judgment of the LORD. The "once-in-a-generation" deep freeze began on January 29th - exactly 7 days after New York's abominable abortion-on-demand bill had become State law. In the Book of Revelation, the number seven is synonymous with God's judgments upon a rebellious world.

The record-shattering cold put God-denying global warming advocates on their heels, and they had tried to come up with every explanation as to why the global cooling was *the result* of global warming. There's just one logical explanation for the Polar Vortex of 2019: a God who *controls the weather* on Earth. Every other explanation falls flat, and any other theory falls apart.

JESUS SAID, WHEN THESE THINGS BEGIN TO COME TO PASS, THEN LOOK UP, AND LIFT UP YOUR HEADS; FOR YOUR REDEMPTION DRAWETH NIGH.

- LUKE 21:28

CHAPTER TWO

MORE SIGNS CONTINUE

JESUS ANSWERED AND SAID UNTO THEM, WHEN IT IS
EVENING, YE SAY, IT WILL BE FAIR WEATHER: FOR THE SKY IS
RED. AND IN THE MORNING, IT WILL BE FOUL WEATHER TO
DAY: FOR THE SKY IS RED AND LOWERING. O YE HYPOCRITES,
YE CAN DISCERN THE FACE OF THE SKY; BUT CAN YE NOT
DISCERN THE SIGNS OF THE TIMES?

- MATTHEW 16:2-3

ABORTION

IN 2018, MORE PEOPLE had died from abortions than any other cause of death in the world - approximately 42-million. There is also a new President at Planned Parenthood, Dr. Leana Wen, who replaced Cecile Richards as head of the nation's largest abortion business. She told *People* magazine that she viewed abortion as "a basic human right." So, much like her predecessor, Wen believes that murdering your child is the "right" of every American.

In 2019, on the 46th Anniversary of the abominable Roe V. Wade SCOTUS decision, New York's Democrat-controlled State legislature and Governor passed a law to enshrine a "fundamental right" to abortion in the State's Constitution. The abominable law wiped out all restrictions on abortions, allowing the procedure to be performed up to birth! It's a license to murder babies without consequence. Other Dem-controlled States followed suit, passing similar bills soon after. Many Dems now embrace *infanticide*.

Under the New York law, non-physicians and midwives can perform abortions, and protections for babies surviving abortion procedures ("born alive") are removed. This means that they can be "left to die" after birth. Not only did the Democrats and their pro-choice supporters express absolutely no remorse, but on the day that the bill was signed into law they publicly *celebrated* it. I warned in my first book that California was at the top of the list to receive judgments from the LORD for many reasons, and later in this book you will read how those judgments have begun to fall. New York is now at the top of the list as well. You cannot shed innocent blood on this earth - let alone *celebrate* shedding it - and expect to escape the consequences of provoking the LORD.

A month after the New York law was passed, 44 Democrat Senators voted against the Born Alive Act. Essentially, they voted to let a baby DIE if born alive after a botched abortion. That is nothing short of Satanic. Also, for the first time in over 150 years, abortion became free and legal in Ireland in 2019. Irish legislature voted to allow a woman to have an abortion into the 12th week of pregnancy. A member of the Irish Parliament, Bríd Smith, said it was "one of those rare moments in life when you feel such joy, the sheer joy of beating back the Church's agenda, really beating it back for once." WOW. Someone taking such delight in making war on the people of God is downright demonic. It is the Book of Revelation playing out before our eyes -

"AND THE DRAGON (SATAN) WAS WROTH WITH THE WOMAN (MARY), AND WENT TO MAKE WAR WITH THE REMNANT OF HER SEED (JESUS), WHICH KEEP THE COMMANDMENTS OF GOD, AND HAVE THE TESTIMONY OF JESUS CHRIST." - REVELATION 12:17

LGBT PRIDE

Since the days of Obama's administration, there have been public libraries across America hosting what is known as "Drag Queen Story Time." During the events, men dressed in drag (even demon costumes) read "Trans" books to young children. As if that were not bad enough, Planned Parenthood and left-wing Human Rights Campaign (HRC) push initiatives in schools that teach kids about masturbation, crossdressing, gay sex, transgenderism, and BDSM in Sex-Ed programs all across the country.

LifeSiteNews recently reported that attacks on Christians by LGBT activists in Canada have significantly escalated. In Alberta, Education Minister David Eggen is threatening to defund or shut down religious schools not accepting Gay-Straight Alliance clubs. The Supreme Court of Canada recently ruled against a Christian university in British Columbia, forbidding that private institution from having students agree to a lifestyle contract when enrolling.

In 2018, Canada's government had forced employers to sign a document indicating they support transgender rights and abortion. If business owners refused, which most (hopefully all) Christians did, then they were denied Canadian Summer Jobs grants. While the Christian-owned organizations were being shut out of the Jobs program, there had been nearly $100,000 in grants awarded to the Canadian organizations affiliated with Planned Parenthood.

Feeling emboldened under their liberal leader, Justin Trudeau, Canada's LGBT activists are now targeting churches - demanding the government strip charitable status from churches disagreeing with their radical ideology. Obviously, *true* Christian churches do (or should). Canadian pro-life activist, Jonathon Van Maren, has warned that the radicals in the LGBT crowd will soon be saying, "Any good that these churches do is vastly outweighed by their fundamental bigotry."

In other shocking news from 2018, it was reported that there was a 4000% increase in kids who identify as transgender. Kids! God help us. That's an ominous sign of the Tribulation coming in the very near future, during which Christians all across the world will be hated even more so than we are now. We will be murdered for our Faith, and thrown into prison, for only believing the Word of God over the opinions and feelings of modern society. Belief in basic human biology - that God created "male and female" - will most likely be a criminal offense. We're not yet in the Tribulation, and transgender activists are already threatening the lives of those refusing to embrace their ideology.

In December of 2018, LGBT radicals threatened the life of a professor in England because she refused to bow to their agenda. *BBC News* reported that a University of Reading professor, Rosa Freedman, received threats of murder and rape. She said that she endured constant online abuse and that her office door had been covered in urine. The threats and hostility started after Freedman publicly discussed a government program that would aid people wanting to change their gender. She opposes the idea that people can choose their gender, believing the Bible's truth that we are all born as one particular gender.

When she had made her way to an event, where she'd discuss proposed changes to the Gender Recognition Act, she was forced to hide in bushes to avoid menacing activists who were following her. Seriously?! It's insane that this can happen in a so-called civil society. A woman is forced to hide from a mob of men because she won't submit to their radical agenda. Where is the #MeToo movement in this case? Does it not count when men making the threats advocate for the LGBT agenda? The Left are hypocrites, and should be ashamed of their egregious double standards.

What's interesting about the modern mob mentality of LGBT activists is that homosexuals we read about in the Bible behaved in the *exact same way*. In Sodom, a mob of them stormed Lot's home in an effort to get their way -

"THE MEN OF THE CITY, EVEN THE MEN OF SODOM, COMPASSED THE HOUSE ROUND, BOTH OLD AND YOUNG, ALL THE PEOPLE FROM EVERY QUARTER: AND THEY CALLED UNTO LOT, AND SAID UNTO HIM, WHERE ARE THE MEN WHICH CAME IN TO YOU THIS NIGHT? BRING THEM OUT UNTO US, THAT WE MAY KNOW (LAY WITH) THEM. AND LOT WENT OUT AT THE DOOR UNTO THEM, AND SHUT THE DOOR AFTER HIM, AND SAID, I PRAY YOU, BRETHREN, DO NOT SO WICKEDLY. BEHOLD NOW, I HAVE TWO DAUGHTERS WHICH HAVE NOT KNOWN MAN; LET ME, I PRAY YOU, BRING THEM OUT UNTO YOU, AND DO YOU TO THEM AS IS GOOD IN YOUR EYES: ONLY UNTO THESE MEN DO NOTHING; FOR THEREFORE CAME THEY UNDER THE SHADOW OF MY ROOF. AND THEY SAID, STAND BACK. AND THEY SAID AGAIN, THIS ONE FELLOW CAME IN TO SOJOURN, AND HE HAS BECOME A JUDGE: NOW WILL WE DEAL WORSE WITH YOU, THAN WITH THEM. AND THEY PRESSED SORE UPON THE MAN, EVEN LOT, AND CAME NEAR TO BREAK THE DOOR. BUT THE MEN (ANGELS) PUT FORTH THEIR HAND, AND PULLED LOT INTO THE HOUSE TO THEM, AND SHUT TO THE DOOR. AND THEY SMOTE THE MEN THAT WERE AT THE DOOR OF THE HOUSE WITH BLINDNESS, BOTH SMALL AND GREAT: SO THAT THEY WEARIED THEMSELVES TO FIND THE DOOR." - GENESIS 19:4-11

Notice how homosexuals, all the way back in that first Book of our Bible, accused Lot of "judging" them. Today, the demonic spirits possessing homosexuals still use the same lines and mob mentality as they did from the very beginning. Freedman said that it was scary to have a mob of students, many of whom were male, following her. She also said that she was explicitly *urged to leave* the university because of her views.

FALLING AWAY FROM THE FAITH

In 2018, "The State of Theology" in America was examined by Ligonier Ministries in a survey conducted by *LifeWay* Research. The survey was based on interviews with 3,000 Americans, and it was the third time that Ligonier and *LifeWay* conducted the study. The others were done in 2014 and 2016. Ligonier said the survey helps uncover what Americans think about God, Jesus Christ, sin, and eternity. As with studies I'd shared in the previous book, the results are alarming and they highlight the *sad state* of Theology in America's churches. While it was a survey of all Americans, I want to zero in on shocking responses by Evangelical Christians.

On the survey statement, "Everyone sins a little, but most are good by nature," 52% of Evangelicals agreed. *More than half* (of what is supposed to be the most Biblically-literate denomination) completely contradict what God's Word teaches. Not one human being on this earth is "good by nature." We live in a fallen world, where we're prone to sin since youth. We are more likely to break God's Moral Law each day than to do good. Like it or not, that is just the way it is. We all sin, and fall short of the Glory of God (Romans 3:23). That's the reason we all need a Saviour. We serve a Holy God, Who cannot dwell in the presence of sin. As long as we're stained in sin, we cannot enter into His Presence. We aren't "good." Every single one of us is a sinner.

The holiest pastor or priest wrestles with sin daily. Agreeing that *most* people are good is 100% against the Bible. Jesus said, when He was called "good," that "there is *none good* but GOD." He was referring to His Father in Heaven, YHWH. Another piece of Scripture, obliterating the view that "most are good," is found in the Book of Romans -

"AS IT IS WRITTEN, THERE IS NONE RIGHTEOUS, NO, NOT ONE: THERE IS NONE THAT UNDERSTANDETH, THERE IS NONE THAT SEEKETH AFTER GOD. THEY ARE ALL GONE OUT OF THE WAY, THEY ARE TOGETHER BECOME UNPROFITABLE; THERE IS NONE THAT DOES GOOD, NO, NOT ONE." - ROMANS 3:10-12

You'd think that would be plain enough to anyone claiming to be a Bible believer, but I guess a lot of Evangelicals today totally glossed over that Chapter of Romans. While it's disappointing for believers to agree with the first statement, their agreeing with the next one is beyond blasphemous. On the statement, "God accepts the worship of all religions," 51% of so-called Christians agreed. Again, more than half! I'm curious as to what version of the Holy Bible that half of Evangelicals are reading (or not reading at all), because their versions are poorly translated. God does *not* accept the worship of other gods or religions in any way, shape, or form. He condemns idolatry all throughout the pages of our Holy Book, in both the Old and New Testaments.

He most assuredly condemns worship of Islam and Allah, as Allah is the "Baal" of our Bible. As I proved in my first book, the Quran is the antithesis of the Holy Bible. The LORD condemns worshipping any false gods, and that would pertain to Buddhism, Hinduism, and all of the other "ism" religions of the world (with the exception of Judaism). YHWH is clear that there is "no other God" but *Him* (Exodus 20:3, Isaiah 44:6-8 and 45:5); and when you put your faith in His Son for your salvation, honoring Jesus equates to honoring Him (Psalms 2:12, John 5:23 and 14:6, Acts 4:12, 1st Corinthians 8:6, 1st John 2:23). He and Lord Jesus are "ONE" (John 1:1, 1:18, 10:30 and 14:9, Isaiah 9:6).

To those 51% of Evangelicals who think that God's okay with us worshipping other gods, or adhering to other religions: you are grossly mistaken. You must have never read the Bible. There is no possible way that you could have. Christians serve one God - the *true God* of Heaven and Earth. There are no others!

FAITHLESS GENERATION

In the same survey, the theological beliefs of everyday Americans were examined. On the statement, "Even the smallest sin deserves eternal damnation," 69% had disagreed - nearly ¾ of Americans! While it may sound harsh to some for me to say that a white lie, gossiping, disrespecting parents, not keeping the Sabbath holy, or coveting property of your neighbor, would result in you having to spend an eternity in Hell... it's 100% *true*. As I said earlier, we all sin. So, it doesn't matter how little or how big a sin we commit. God is Holy - we are unholy. Therefore, based on our own merits, we can not stand in His Presence unless we accept His prescribed solution to this problem: JESUS.

He Who knew no sin bore the punishment of sin for us, and died for every one that we have committed - or will ever commit. He suffered the just judgment we deserved, so that we unworthy sinners could spend eternity in Heaven. If you don't accept Jesus' sacrifice on your behalf, then, yes, even the smallest of sins will sentence you to eternal damnation. The LORD has made a way so that you would not have to endure the consequences of your sins; but if you don't repent and accept Christ as Saviour, *you condemn yourself* to Hell - not God.

On the statement, "Religious belief is a matter of personal opinion; it is not about objective truth," 60% agreed. The Bible was penned by the Holy Spirit of God. It is the only real *truth* in this life. If you believe God's Word, then you believe the truth. Something that billions of people around the globe have believed for thousands of years, which has always held true and has never been proven false, cannot be considered a personal *opinion*. 60% of Americans are dead wrong (Psalms 119:160, John 8:32, 15:26, 16:13 and 17:17, 2nd Peter 1:21).

Even worse news, coming out of the survey, is that the trend of wider acceptance of same-sex relations continues. For the first time, in nearly a 5-year period of surveys, more Americans (than not) agree that the Bible's teaching on same-sex relationships is "outdated." On the statement, "The Holy Bible's condemnation of homosexual behavior doesn't apply today," 44% agreed. Though every reference to homosexuality in the Bible is clear (in both Old and New Testaments) that it is abominable sin in the eyes of the LORD, many Americans don't believe God cares too much about the issue in our day. They couldn't be more wrong. The rebellion of the homosexual community against Almighty God is bringing judgment after judgment upon this backslidden nation.

On the statement, "The Holy Bible is 100% accurate in all it teaches," only 50% agreed. *Half of Americans* do not believe the Bible to be the Word of God! What a disgusting shame. Anything that can be proven about the Bible has been, or is being proved. Anything that has not... *will be*. On the flipside, nothing has ever been disproven that has been recorded in the Holy Bible. *Nothing*. I, for one, will continue to trust the inerrancy of God's Word over the fallible *opinions* of men.

Finally, as to how young adults (Millennials) responded to the survey... just as you would expect... *not good*. On the statement, "The Bible is not literally true," 53% agreed. That is up 7% from the 2016 survey. On the statement, "Gender identity is a matter of choice," 46% agreed. Even though we were all created with either male or female anatomy, they're saying we can *choose* the gender we *prefer*. This absurd ideology is antithetical to God's Word.

Sadly, it appears the State of Theology in America is getting worse year after year. People are far more concerned with being entertained in church today, rather than learning something about God. They want "feel good" time, and never "reflect and repent" time. Hopefully, those of us who faithfully preach God's truth to a backslidden nation and world will never grow weary. We need to shout His Word from the rooftops, whether people want to hear it or not; because many want to call themselves "Christian," while cooking up their *own* ideas about what the Faith is about. They are transforming Christianity into what they believe that it *should* be, as opposed to what it always *has been* and *is*.

Just like our Lord and God in Heaven, the Word of the LORD is *the same yesterday, today, and forever.* God doesn't allow us to change it to better suit mainstream opinions of any generation. As a matter of fact, He forbids it (Deuteronomy 4:2 and Revelation 22:18-19). His Word has stood the test of time for good reason - because it endures *forever* (Isaiah 40:8, Matthew 24:35, 1st Peter 1:25). You are entitled to believe whatever it is you choose in this life; but if what you're believing is not in line with what the Bible says, then you're believing a LIE. Like it or not.

JESUS SAID, WHEN YE SHALL SEE ALL THESE THINGS, KNOW THAT IT (RAPTURE) IS NEAR, EVEN AT THE DOORS.

- MATTHEW 24:33

CHAPTER THREE

MASS SHOOTINGS

IN THE LAST DAYS PERILOUS TIMES SHALL COME.

- 2ND TIMOTHY 3:1

POLITICAL POINTS OF VIEW are all that we ever seem to hear in debates and discussions about mass shootings, and very rarely do we hear a Biblical perspective. I intend to change that.

If you're a Democrat, you probably think that mass shootings have increased under President Trump and that the solution is *gun control*. If you're Republican, you likely believe the tragic events began to increase under his predecessor, Barack Obama, and that *more guns* are the answer - not less. Well, you'd both be wrong. Mass shootings in America had become more frequent and more deadly over time, starting in 1999. I think it's very interesting that the year includes 6-6-6 upside down. That just so happened to be the year of the infamous Columbine High School shooting. The perpetrators of that attack were two atheist students who had been inspired by Adolph Hitler. The depraved souls murdered a dozen fellow students and one teacher.

A Faith-based film was made about the tragedy and centered on one of the victims, devout Christian Rachel Joy Scott. Masey Mclain portrayed Scott in *I'm Not Ashamed*. If you have not yet seen the film, then I highly recommend it as a must-see. The two demonic shooters carried out the attack on April 20th, which just so happened to be Hitler's birthday. Over the course of the next 2 decades, as the nation drifted further and further away from God, more demonically influenced youth had followed in the footsteps of the Columbine shooters.

In 2005, a 16-year-old had murdered 7 in Minnesota. In 2007, a 23-year-old student murdered 33 at Virginia Tech University. It became the deadliest school shooting in U.S. history. In 2012, a 20-year-old had shot up an Elementary School in Connecticut. He murdered 26. 20 of the victims were children, aged 6-7 years old. In 2014, a student murdered 4 fellow students in Washington. In 2015, a student in Oregon had murdered 8 students and a teacher. In 2018, a 15-year-old slaughtered 2 and injured 18 in Kentucky. In the same year, a 19-year-old student went on a shooting spree at his former high school in Florida - murdering 17. Three months later, another black-hearted teen shot up a High School in Texas. His cold-blooded attack left 10 dead.

It is no surprise that all the young shooters had one thing in common: anti-God influences. The Florida shooter tortured small animals, was anti-Semitic, and testified that demons spoke to him. The Texas shooter idolized the Columbine psychopaths, wearing a long black trench coat just like theirs. His social media accounts revealed that he, too, was fond of Hitler, as his clothing had been adorned with Nazi, Communist, Fascist, and Occult symbols. He said that he had attributed his "evil side" to the demon Baphomet in one social media post. These demonic kids are the consequence of children not being taught the Laws of God regarding right and wrong, and it's no coincidence that the *least Christian generation* in U.S. history is the most violent.

In my first book, I shared a study revealing more teenagers than ever before identify as atheists - and that only 4% of today's youth hold a Biblical worldview. Yet, people wonder why schools have turned into war zones! I guarantee mass shootings in schools will continue, and may even get worse. It won't matter how many gun restriction laws are passed. As long as the hearts of the youth are evil, Satan will lead their hands to a weapon. There's only one solution that'll work to put an end to America's school shootings epidemic, and that's to put Almighty God back in schools - where He rightfully belongs.

Today, far too many Americans are ignorant to the fact that America's first schoolbook was the Holy Bible. Ever since it was forced out, along with prayer, the public school environment has rapidly become less safe. In a 1940 survey of school teachers, the top disciplinary problems were: talking out of turn, chewing gum, running in the halls, and dress-code violations. Flash-forward to 2019, and you can see just what America's downward spiral away from the LORD has done to our nation's school system. The top problems that teachers of this generation report are: drug/alcohol abuse, pregnancy, suicide, rape, robbery, assault, and shootings.

Things are unquestionably worse in schools than they've ever been in the history of the USA. Examining history, we find only *one thing* has changed over the course of the past two centuries. At America's founding, did our forefathers own guns? How about in 1940? The answer is yes, on both counts. Did young boys have hormones back then, and desire intimate relations with girls? Yes. Did alcohol exist back then? Yup. So, why no mass shootings in schools? How come as many young girls weren't being raped, or getting pregnant? Why no assault in schools? Why no widespread alcohol use amongst the youth? What was so different throughout the first few centuries of the United States? The universal answer to all of these hows and whys is FEAR OF GOD.

Not only was the Lord revered above all, but kids were taught Godly morals from a young age; and God's Word was central to our nation's education system. Teens back then could have never imagined doing abominable things that today's kids do. Yet, here we are… no God in our schools, coupled with a young generation inundated daily with lust - gratuitous violence - the normalization of drug and alcohol use - immorality - blasphemy - even a bitter hostility toward the God of our fathers - and how can anyone be surprised by where we are as a society? Just examine the history of mass shootings in America; and it is plain to see that after the LORD was pushed out, *evil* has filled the void.

In the 50-year period from 1948-1998, there were TEN mass shootings with about 150 victims. From 1999-2018, which is less than half the previous period, there were 19 mass shootings with about 375 victims. In under half the time, shootings have nearly *doubled* and the lives lost have *more than doubled*! Still, liberals would rather blame Almighty God for America's ills; rather than acknowledge that we need Him more than ever.

In 2015, a deranged gunman shot up a Planned Parenthood in Colorado - murdering 3 people. As soon as the incident began to headline the major news networks, I knew the lamestream media would demonize Christians because of our strong stance against the baby-murdering organization. As expected, before any details of the shooter had been revealed, the media, Planned Parenthood, left-wing pundits, and liberal keyboard warriors, had labeled the gunman a "right-wing pro-life extremist." Even after the identity of the shooter was revealed, proving he was not a Christian, they continued to place blame on the "extreme" and "hateful" ideology of "conservative Christians."

The shooter was *anything but* a staunch Holy Bible-believing Christian. He was, instead, a mentally ill veteran with a lengthy criminal record. Still, lefties pushed the narrative that us pro-lifers were *extremists*. First of all, you can't be pro-life and a murderer. That would be an oxymoron. Second, you cannot be a *defender* of life, while at the same time, *destroying* life. So, it was nauseating to watch the liberals (who advocate for taking the lives of unborn babies on a daily basis) accuse the pro-life movement of bearing a responsibility for the senseless murder. Most Christians strongly oppose Planned Parenthood, yes, but we *never* call for violence against them or their employees. We never have. We never will. If you do, then you just aren't a true Christian.

There is no justification in the Bible for taking innocent lives (Exodus 20:13, Numbers 35:30, Matthew 19:18). While many in the Planned Parenthood organization are Godless, and downright evil, we must leave vengeance to God alone. We are never to take justice into our own hands. Unless someone is attempting to do you or your family life-threatening harm, it cannot be considered justice to take the life of another human being. I do not care how evil that you may think the other person is - the fate of their life is not in your hands, but in God's. If He wants to punish them for their sins, you can be absolutely sure that He will. It is not our job to execute His judgment.

That is precisely why Christians oppose Planned Parenthood as passionately as we do, because their hands shed innocent blood *every day*. They are responsible for cutting short the lives of over 7-million children of God, and they'll have to answer to Him for it someday. Sadly, they see nothing wrong with murdering babies; but they sure seem to find a heck of a lot wrong with God-fearing Christians. Planned Parenthood's Executive Vice President, Dawn Laguens, released a statement in wake of the Colorado shooting, saying, "One of the lessons of this awful tragedy is that words matter, and that hateful rhetoric fuels violence." Obviously, she was referring to us Christians who regularly speak out against the murder of the unborn.

She added, "It's not enough to denounce the tragedy without also denouncing the poisonous rhetoric that fueled it." Notice that she did not once blame the lunatic who actually murdered three people at the clinic, including a *Christian* cop. She, instead, used the tragedy as a means to demonize her organization's outspoken adversaries. Do you think she would have lashed out at Muslims, or criticized the dangerous rhetoric of the Quran, had the shooter been Islamic? I highly doubt it.

Following any Islamic terror attack, of which there have been far too many to count in the past decade, the lamestream media and the libs come to the defense of Muslims. They say that *not all* Muslims are terrorists, and urge others to not condemn an entire religion due to the actions of *a few*. Yet, when a deranged white guy - neither Christian nor pro-life - shoots up an abortion clinic, the same liberals say, "ALL Christians are extremists and Biblical beliefs are dangerous." Talk about a double standard!

In June of 2016, an Islamic terrorist shot up a gay nightclub in Orlando, Florida, known as The Pulse. In the brutal massacre, about 50 were murdered and over 50 more wounded. At that time, it was the deadliest mass shooting in U.S. history. The shooter, Omar Mateen, called 911 during the attack to publicly declare his allegiance to the ISIS (Islamic State) terror group. A spokesman for the group had called for attacks against Americans during the Muslim holiday of Ramadan, which began just a few days earlier. Mainstream media had dubbed 30-year-old Mateen "mentally ill," conveniently ignoring his Islamic ties. Targeting homosexuals for death was not some new idea cooked up by Mateen. Just like the targeting of Jews and Christians, it is called for in Islam's Quran.

In Islamic nations like Afghanistan, Iran, Mauritania, Nigeria, Saudi Arabia, Somalia, Sudan, the UAE, and Yemen, homosexual activity carries a death penalty. What a contrast with the teachings of Christianity, the Faith which the LGBT community attacks the most. Followers of Christ simply speak out against homosexuality and same-sex marriage, while followers of Muhammad set out to abolish homosexuals by deadly force. Lord Jesus commanded us to show poor sinners the error of their ways, to preach repentance, and lead them to Him. Muhammad, on the other hand, commands his followers to torture, terrorize, and murder them.

I once heard it said, concerning the difference between those who murder in Allah's name and those who murder in the Name of Jesus, "Muslims who murder for the cause of Allah are being *good* Muslims, but Christians who murder for the cause of Christ are being *bad* Christians." Amen. 100% true. So, while the LGBT activists sure do seem to hate Bible thumpers like me, they should be extremely thankful that I'm not thumping a Quran!

In 2017, the toll of a mass shooting in Nevada surpassed that of the Florida nightclub massacre - making it America's deadliest. A 64-year-old, Stephen Paddock, shot dead about 60 people, and injured 500+ others at an outdoor concert. The Route 91 Harvest Festival, which took place just outside Mandalay Bay Resort and Casino in Las Vegas, drew nearly 25,000 concertgoers - making it the perfect target for a demonic madman seeking to end multiple lives. Paddock opened fire on the crowd from a 32nd floor room of the Mandalay Bay Hotel. About 20 weapons were found in his room, including 10 rifles. It was obviously a premeditated attack.

He began shooting during a performance by a country music singer, Jason Aldean, who was closing act of the Festival. After Aldean was rushed off stage, chaos ensued. Thousands of people began to panic, running for cover, and trampling one another in a stampede-like atmosphere. The Mandalay Bay Hotel, from where Paddock had fired, was across the street from the concert venue. It is believed that he fired from 2 different rooms to get different angles on victims. His brother, Eric Paddock, told reporters that he had "no religious affiliation and no political affiliation."

Just one month after the Vegas slaughter, a church in Texas was targeted. A 26-year-old avowed atheist, Devin Patrick Kelley, opened fire on the congregation of a Baptist Church in Sutherland Springs - murdering over two dozen and injuring 20 others. It was the deadliest mass shooting in the State, and deadliest shooting in an American place of worship in modern history.

Mass shootings are not always defined by law enforcement as acts of terrorism, but they most certainly are. In a mass shooting, just as in an act of terror, a perpetrator is seeking to end as many lives as possible. And just like with terrorism, as I pointed out in my previous book, mass shootings are not about guns or "mental health." They are the unfortunate result of men not knowing God. When there is no God in the heart of man, evil will always thrive. Whether it be an atheist or Islamic terrorist, evil men are prone to commit murder. Mass shooters are under the influence of Satan. In John 8:44, Lord Jesus said, "You are of your father the devil, and the lusts of your father you will do. He was a *murderer* from the beginning."

Liberals and Democrats who use deadly tragedies to push for gun control obviously don't read the Holy Bible. The gun control argument is always made by people who don't seem to believe in the age-old spiritual battle of good vs. evil and God vs. the devil. In this politically correct nation, liberals don't want to believe that Satan works in the hearts of unbelievers. That doesn't change the fact that he most certainly does. Murder is an abomination to the LORD. Since the irreligious people don't believe in the God who created a moral law, they have nothing that prevents them from committing immoral acts.

Thus, I do not believe that guns have anything whatsoever to do with the plague of mass shootings in America. I believe that the absence of God, in the hearts and lives of many of our fellow citizens, has absolutely *everything* to do with it. I get so disgusted when I hear liberals say, "we don't need prayers, we need action" in the wake of mass shootings. It is that Godless attitude that is allowing demonic murderers to flourish in our society. There is absolutely no legislation that politicians can pass to prevent the deadly incidents in the future. But seeking the LORD in fervent prayer can prevent any and all evil acts.

Liberals can ban every gun in America, and the result would be "mass stabbings." Confiscate every knife, and evil men would use pressure cookers or vehicles to take countless lives. You can never stop demonic men from harming others by just taking away their weapons of choice. Murderers will find a way to murder. Do y'all remember Cain and Abel? Will we ever ban *stones*? In order to stop the senseless bloodshed of mass shootings once and for all, it is not the minds of men that need to change - nor the size of the guns that they are allowed to own. It is their *hearts*. And there is only *one way* to change them... It isn't psychiatry. It isn't gun control. It's JESUS, and Jesus Christ *alone*.

EVEN AS THEY DID NOT LIKE TO RETAIN GOD IN THEIR KNOWLEDGE, GOD GAVE THEM OVER TO A REPROBATE MIND, TO DO THOSE THINGS WHICH ARE NOT CONVENIENT; BEING FILLED WITH ALL UNRIGHTEOUSNESS... WICKEDNESS... MALICIOUSNESS... MURDER... MALIGNITY.

- ROMANS 1:28-29

CHAPTER FOUR

RACISM

FOR THE LORD SEETH NOT AS MAN SEETH; FOR MAN
LOOKETH ON THE OUTWARD APPEARANCE, BUT THE LORD
LOOKETH ON THE HEART.

- 1ST SAMUEL 16:7

IN ALL MY YEARS of writing, I have only touched on the issue
of racism a few times. This is because I do not believe that we can
ever eradicate the disgusting ideology by paying its adherents, or
their hateful rhetoric, any attention. Unfortunately, with the rise
of social media in our day and age - which has given a platform to
the dregs of our society - hate for others based on their skin color
has spread like a plague. So, just as I had felt that the Lord called
me to address the hot-button issues of our day - such as abortion
and LGBT Pride - from a Biblical perspective in my last book, I
believe that He has now led me to tackle this issue.

I will not be addressing this issue from the right or left side of
the political aisle either, though it is well known that I lean to the
"right" politically as a staunch conservative Christian. I think that
the term "right-wing" has been hijacked; because there are far too
many unabashed racists claiming to belong to the right side of the
political aisle. They most certainly don't belong there. That is not
to say that the left doesn't have their share of racists on the fringe

of the Democrat Party, because they absolutely do. The brands of racism are different on the opposite ends of the political spectrum, but should all be condemned exactly the same.

Unfortunately, one form of racism is far too prevalent on both sides of the aisle - anti-Semitism. There are the Jew-hating White Supremacists of the alt-right, and the anti-Israel Muslims on the hard-left. Both Republican and Democrat parties would be wise to condemn them loudly and often. I had addressed the scourge of anti-Semitism in my first book, so take a moment to read it if you haven't already. In this chapter, I'm going to focus on other forms of racism that are rife in our nation today. For starters, there are whites and black Christians peddling some racially-divisive belief systems; and so I must question their faith. Because I don't think a true believer in Christ could ever see another human "in color."

Our God is *colorblind*. Thus, as His children, we are called to be too. The LORD looks on the hearts of men, and never on the shades of their skin. From the beginning, He has only viewed the human race in two ways - as either believers or unbelievers. You either choose to serve the true God of Heaven and Earth, or you choose to follow false gods. You do one or the other. There is no in the middle. When you do the first, it does not matter if you are white, black, brown, red, or yellow, God knows you and you are His child. If you do the latter, being light-skinned or dark-skinned doesn't matter in the slightest to the LORD. He *doesn't* know you and you are a stranger to Him. All that ever matters to Him is obedience to His Word and to His will.

If you're defiant and don't accept His Son's sacrifice on your behalf, as atonement for your disobedience, then being born white or black cannot save you. You are going to Hell. Plain and simple. In the end, we will all be judged on our faith alone. Nothing else. We will not be judged in regard to how much money we made, nor by how many kids we had raised; not by worldly positions we held, nor by the size of our homes or businesses; not by how kind or generous we were to others, nor by any good deeds which we had done. The *only thing* that the LORD will care about, come Judgment Day, is whether or not you believed in the Lord Jesus Christ to reconcile your unholy soul unto your Holy Creator.

Today, there are believers all around the world - from every nation, culture, tribe, and color. When we are "in Christ," we are *all equal* in God's Sight. I am not any more favored by the Lord than an African believer, Jewish believer, Arab believer, Spanish believer, or Asian believer. We are all "one race" in Christ Jesus. We're all one family. We're all members of the Church, regardless of denomination. We are all members of one body, of which He is "the Head" (Romans 12:4-5, 1st Corinthians 10:16-17 and 12:12, Ephesians 1:22 - 2:19-22 - 4:15-16 - 5:23, Colossians 1:18).

Though I am a white man, I might actually have more black men and women as my "brothers and sisters" than other whites. Whosoever is washed and covered in the Blood of God's Son is my family. Whosoever isn't is *not* my brother or sister. They are strangers. A black believer in Christ, who believes every word of the Bible as strongly as I do, is more so family to me than a blood relative who doesn't believe. That's why I, personally, never view others in color. My Faith prevents me from doing so. For there is no skin color that makes any of us superior over another.

Our God wills that all men and women, everywhere - and of every color - would come to Him through His Son, the Prince of Peace. Only then can we experience lasting peace and equality in our divided nation and world. These two long-sought-after things can never be obtained through any government, political leaders, laws, or affirmative action, but are only found in God alone. The ever-growing racial tension that's been sweeping the nation is just one of the many consequences of forcing God out of America - at a time when we need Him more than ever.

As believers, we must not grow weary in preaching His Word - whether our fellow citizens want to hear it or not. If we sit back, resigned to the belief that things will never change, and keep the LORD's unifying message of salvation all to ourselves or only to our churches... America may soon find itself in another Civil War.

We must perpetually place our Faith above our race. Because if any Holy Bible believer is placing their race over the Faith, then their faith is meaningless. You and I are *Christians* above all else. That label should be setting us apart from every other group in the world. We should never be engaged in "race wars," and never be members of race-based groups - especially not those who engage in violent protests or unruly riots to make their voices heard. We should never be known for being Caucasian or African American; nor for being Asian, Hispanic, Indian, Native American, or any other ethnicity. We should be known as Christians. Period. The only race that's ever had a special place in God's heart is the Jew. The rest of us are simply known to Him as "Gentiles."

If we ever had to fill out paperwork in Heaven, and there was a "race" section, I suspect that there would only be two options - Jew or Gentile. And the LORD wills that *both* would be united in Christ, King of the Jews and Savior of the world. In the Kingdom of God, there will be no "White Power" or "Black Power." There will only be "Power in the Blood of Jesus." These words might pain the White Supremacists or Black Liberation Theologists, but everything I'm teaching is 100% Biblical. It's the Word of God. It is not my own. Godless men like Richard Spencer, Al Sharpton (who is no "Reverend"), and Louis Farrakhan believe God should favor them (and all those who look like them) because they think that their particular race is superior to all others.

These men, and people who follow their abhorrent doctrines, are of the devil. There is no nice way to say it. Richard Spencer is a neo-Nazi White Supremacist, and is the leader of the "alt-right" movement. He is also an atheist. That explains why he so strongly rejects the traditional "right-wing," especially those belonging to the Christian Right (like myself). Spencer says that "White people should have their own nation, separate from the people of colour." Sadly, as America has increasingly become a Biblically-illiterate nation, he's amassed thousands of followers across the country. A majority of them are anti-Semitic members of the KKK (Ku Klux Klan), neo-Nazis, White Supremacists, and White Nationalists.

Stirring up the racial strife on the other end of the political spectrum are men like Al Sharpton and Farrakhan. These men are the dark-skinned equivalents of Spencer, as they have both made highly controversial statements about Jews and whites. Sharpton has made a career out of profiting off of racial injustices done to African Americans hundreds of years ago, while Farrakhan leads the Nation of Islam and is an unrepentant Jew-hater. Sadly, much like Spencer, they've both accumulated very large cult followings. Sharpton masquerades as a man of God, but is nothing more than a money-hungry race hustler and a habitual blasphemer. He often compares Jesus Christ to young criminals who are shot by police for resisting arrest.

Jesus was *no* criminal. He was falsely accused of being one, and was crucified for the crimes He didn't commit alongside real criminals. To compare Him (the Savior of the world) to immoral, drug-dealing, gun-toting thugs is beyond blasphemous. Sharpton has even said that certain books of the Bible should be "thrown out" because he says they "condone" slavery. He obviously didn't study the Biblical languages of Hebrew or Greek in Theological School. If he did, then he'd know that "slaves" and "servants" in the Bible were *not* the same as African slaves of the 18th-19th Centuries. Not at all the same.

The only real slaves we read about in the Holy Bible were the Hebrew Jews in Egypt. Any other time that you ever read about slaves in God's Word, they were what we know today as butlers or maids. They were indentured servants. They were paid wages for their work, and were not whipped nor bound in chains. After the years of their service were complete, they had the choice to go free or to remain with their masters. To say in any way that the Bible condones slavery, as we know it today, is just plain wrong and is theologically irresponsible. If Sharpton truly were a man of God, and sincerely cared about the "equal" treatment of all God's children, then He'd preach everything I'm teaching. He does not.

Instead, he cherry-picks verses from the Holy Bible to fit his racially-divisive agenda. He is also a teacher of "Black Liberation Theology," which just so happens to be pro-Islam and anti-Israel. Bible believers could never hate God's Chosen Nation or support their enemies. Never. Al Sharpton is nothing but a sham. It's such a shame that men like him and the anti-Christian Malcolm X are widely respected, and even adored, in the black community. They have both long been portrayed as champions in the fight against racism. Yet, in reality, they are both the biggest inciters of it!

Malcolm X was spokesman for the Nation of Islam, the black Muslim movement now led by Farrakhan. He and his followers violently rejected Judeo-Christian America, preaching *supremacy* of blacks over whites. Sadly, much of today's black generation is enamored with X's riotous "by any means necessary" approach to fighting racism - as opposed to Martin Luther King Jr.'s "weapons of love." King preached messages like "Darkness cannot drive out darkness, only light can do that. Hate cannot drive out hate, only love can do that." Meanwhile, Malcolm said that "You don't have a peaceful revolution. You don't have a turn-the-cheek revolution. There is no such thing as a nonviolent revolution."

Which of these two famous Civil Rights leaders do you think that Lord Jesus would approve of? If you have to think about your answer for more than a second, then you haven't read your Bible. Unfortunately, most of the young blacks today appear to side with X over King. Just look at the slogan of the popular Black Lives Matter movement: "No Justice - No Peace." If King were alive today, I believe that his message to this group would be:

No one whom I call a friend would ever say black lives don't matter. All lives matter to God. The trouble with groups like BLM is that their riotous and violent methods are not doing anything to unite this country. They actually only push us further apart. BLM is no better than Richard Spencer's racist alt-right Nazis. Instead of taking a cue from Jesus and Dr. King - to drive out darkness with light and hate with love - BLM activists, instead, burn down buildings, destroy property, assault those who disagree, and clash with police. Their desired end *does not* justify their means.

The Black Lives Matter movement isn't actually about "black lives," believe it or not. They're a radical left-wing group, who are using race as an excuse to push demonic agendas. They support the BDS (Boycott, Divestment, and Sanctions) movement, which supports Palestinian terror against Israel and is for the destruction of the Jewish State. Their Mission Statement states that they are "committed to disrupting nuclear family structure requirement." So, they are against the Biblical family model - Father (Husband), Mother (Wife), and children. Fatherless homes and abortion are big reasons why inner-city black communities have seen so much crime in this nation. Yet, BLM *supports both*. They also push the radical LGBT agenda, "fostering a queer-affirming network."

BLM keeps racism alive and well in this country, as they put blacks into their own category - just like the KKK puts whites in their own category. This should not be so. If they truly wanted all people to be equal, in order to make MLK's dream a reality, then they would stop alienating themselves as "others." As I previously stated, the LORD doesn't see any of us in color! So, why then do we focus so much on the shades of our skin? If you're a Bible believer, you're my brother or sister. The complexion of your skin has no bearing on that whatsoever. Sadly, in a Biblically-illiterate nation and world, not everyone thinks like I do; and not everyone knows our God. Thus, there will always be racists until our Lord comes back down. It is an unfortunate reality.

We Christians cannot change every heart in this world, but we should be placing our focus on the ones we can. Our God is Love. There is no hate in Him. Hate is of Satan. Racism is the epitome of hatred. If we ever want to begin eradicating racism, we need to stop giving a platform to the race-baiters. The lamestream media needs to focus much less on dividers like Richard Spencer or Al Sharpton, and turn their attention to the one true *Uniter* - the Lord Jesus Christ. Everyone needs to stop with the White Pride, Black Pride, Spanish Pride, and every other "Pride"! Because, like hate, pride is of the devil.

As believers, we are all only *one color* in God's sight - RED. That's the color of His Son's sinless Blood - that was shed *for all* on Calvary's Cross, regardless of your skin color. The same Holy Blood that washes, cleanses, covers, and saves me, does the exact same for you. So, let us begin to see one another as our Heavenly Father sees us - as *Family*. We're brothers and sisters in Christ, so let's start acting like it. When we are *in Him*, we are not white or black; and our identities aren't found in being American, African, Asian, European, Middle Eastern, Spanish, nor anything else for that matter. WE'RE CHRISTIAN. That's *all that matters* to God.

FOR YE ARE ALL THE CHILDREN OF GOD BY FAITH IN CHRIST JESUS. FOR AS MANY OF YOU AS HAVE BEEN BAPTIZED INTO CHRIST HAVE PUT ON CHRIST. THERE IS NEITHER JEW NOR GREEK, NEITHER BOND NOR FREE, NEITHER MALE NOR FEMALE: FOR YE ARE ALL ONE IN CHRIST JESUS.

- GALATIANS 3:26-28

CHAPTER FIVE

HISTORIC WILDFIRES

THE FIRE HATH DEVOURED THE PASTURES OF THE
WILDERNESS, AND THE FLAME HATH BURNED ALL THE TREES
OF THE FIELD.

- JOEL 1:19

THE SECULAR MAINSTREAM MEDIA news outlets had found
it difficult to describe the historic wildfire outbreaks of 2017-2018
without using Biblical phrases depicting the End Times. Some of
the headlines catching my eye were: *Apocalyptic - Armageddon is
on - Hell on Earth - Is the World Ending or Something?* Not one
of these headlines came from Bible-based news sites, but were all
found on secular news sites that are normally known for mocking
God. The LORD certainly has His way of getting the attention of
even the most hardened skeptics.

While most "Last Days" scoffers say that there have *always*
been wildfires in California, outbreaks of the past two years were
dubbed as unusual, unprecedented, the deadliest, the largest, and
most destructive in State history. While wildfires are common in
States like Alaska, Arizona, California, Florida, Georgia, Idaho,
Kansas, Mississippi, Missouri, Montana, Nevada, North Carolina,
Oklahoma, Oregon, South Dakota, Texas, and Washington, some
of the absolute worst in U.S. history have occurred only in *our*

generation. 7 out of 9, or 77.7%, of this country's worst wildfires since 1900 have come within the past fifteen years. I am sure that many of you who read my last book just got goosebumps when seeing that percentage.

As I explained in *The Signs of Our Times*, 777 is attributed to our God and Father in Heaven, YHWH, for so many reasons. It is also attributed to His Father/Son relationship with our Lord Jesus Christ. Whenever I see the number 777, I know that God's Hand is at work. The fact that this number popped up so many times, in relation to rare events that have been occurring in our lifetimes - especially within the last two decades - leads me to suspect that YHWH's Son is at the gates and ready to make His return. Come quickly Lord Jesus. Marana tha!

The top seven worst years for wildfires, since 1980, have all come after 2007. They were 2007, 2008, 2011, 2012, 2015, 2017, and 2018. Anyone else notice the correlation between the years that the United States began turning away from God (more than ever before) and the years wildfires got worse? Like other historic disasters that have recently devastated the USA, you can directly connect the time frame of America's falling away from the LORD to the worst wildfires in our nation's history. And it is not climate change, though Godless liberals would like you to believe it is. In reality, it's God's judgment. It is the consequence of rejecting His Word, forgetting His Laws, and widespread blasphemy.

Both 2017 and 2018 greatly eclipsed this decade's average of 6-million acres burned per year. Roughly 10-million acres of land had been burned across the U.S., and over 3-million acres burned in California alone. In the fall of 2017, there were about a dozen wildfires burning out of control in California. Tens of thousands were evacuated, and thousands of structures were destroyed. Two of the State's largest fires, "Tubbs" and "Atlas," burned an area of wine country 3-times larger than Washington, DC. At their peak, the wildfires were advancing at a rate of more than a football field "every three seconds." A State of Emergency had been declared in affected counties, and President Donald Trump had declared a Major Disaster in the State.

Significant damage was done to at least a dozen wineries, and seven pot farms were completely destroyed. Alcohol and drug use are consistently condemned in God's Word, so I don't believe that these locations were burned by chance. In 2018, Cali experienced its most destructive wildfire outbreak on record. During summer, nearly 20 wildfires burned across the State. The biggest of them, "Mendocino Complex Fire," became the largest wildfire in State history. The blaze consisted of two fires, the "Ranch" and "River" Fires, in northern California. The flames had burned over 450,000 acres. At the same time, the "Carr Fire" burned 230,000 acres in Redding, California.

A record-breaking *Flame Tornado*, dubbed the "Fire Whirl," had sprung up near Redding. The tornado was measured as an F-3 - virtually unheard of in California. The State had not recorded a tornado of that strength in 40 years. President Trump declared a Major Disaster in the State once again. A few months later, in the fall of 2018, the next wildfire outbreak was described in headlines as "Hell on Earth." It consisted of three large fires - "Camp, Hill, and Woolsey." The fast-moving blazes caused evacuations of tens of thousands in north and south Cali, including the home city of Godless celebrities - Malibu. Numerous celebrity homes had been damaged or destroyed, including the home of Miley Cyrus.

The "Camp Fire" in northern California had literally burned Paradise to the ground. The town was home to 30,000 people. Cal Fire Captain Scott McLean said, "The community of Paradise is destroyed, it's that kind of devastation." Thousands of homes and businesses were destroyed, and a State of Emergency had been declared for Butte County - where Paradise was located. The fire grew uncontrollably, at a rate of 80 football fields per minute. The inferno scorched over 150,000 acres, and it became the deadliest and most destructive fire in State history.

The other two fires had been sparked in Ventura County. The "Hill Fire" originated about 10 miles northwest from the scene of a mass shooting that occurred just one night earlier in the city of Thousand Oaks. The raging flames rolled down the hills and over the 101 Freeway, which had prompted mandatory evacuations for Cal State University campus. The "Woolsey Fire" was sparked at Woolsey Canyon, and burned across the counties of Ventura and Los Angeles. The fire caused authorities to order the mandatory evacuation of the entire city of Malibu. 100,000 acres of land had been burned, and over 1500 homes were destroyed in the blaze.

I believe that Paradise being destroyed in Cali was symbolic. As a majority of the State have turned their backs on the God of gods, how can we be shocked that *Paradise* was taken away from them and their State was turned into a literal *Hell*? And one night after a mass shooting in the State, after countless liberals said "we don't need prayers - we need gun control," they found themselves in desperate need of prayers. The Hill Fire raged only 10 miles from the site of that shooting. Poetic justice? It is unfortunate that today's liberals want absolutely nothing to do with God, until He literally brings Hell on Earth to their doorsteps. Then they are all about "thoughts and prayers." Well, at least some seemed to be.

Others had lashed out at the LORD for bringing the overdue judgments upon California. The heathen dwelling on the earth in the Book of Revelation mirror this Godless generation perfectly. John prophesied, that during the 7-year Tribulation Hour, instead of repenting when the LORD's judgments fall, the inhabitants of Earth will actually "blaspheme" His Name and "curse" Him. This generation is the first in American history to actually *fulfill* these unimaginable prophecies. God help us.

Too many liberals attribute the record-breaking disasters that America has experienced, throughout the past decade, to a ticked off "Mother Nature." By doing so, they just anger our Father in Heaven all the more. There is no such thing as Mother Nature! The Father alone is the Author of the rare, historic, and unnatural weather we've experienced. It is not *global warming,* and it is not *climate change.* It's the work of a God who makes the impossible possible, who does whatever He wants - whenever He wants - and who never leaves the wicked unpunished. Articles that I'd penned about the California wildfires on my website, *BiblicalSigns.com*, were widely mocked by faithless liberals because I attributed the blazes to His judgment upon the most Godless State in our Union.

Libs believe that the historic fires in Cali were all randomly caused by climate change, and that they had absolutely nothing to do with Californians breaking just about every Law in God's Holy Book. Well, to all who mocked me for calling it the long overdue judgment of God upon the modern-day Sodom and Gomorrah of our nation: I do not think it is a coincidence that the deadliest, the most destructive, and largest, wildfires in the history of California had all occurred in the *exact same year* that the State government attempted to BAN THE BIBLE. How can anyone, believer or not, ignore that undeniable connection?

In my previous book, I warned that California was at the top of the list for coming judgments of the LORD; and I do not take pleasure in saying that I told you so. I wish that all of the heathen in Cali would repent and return to their Maker. He doesn't want to judge them anymore than I want to see them hurt or lose their homes. But the sad and simple fact is that they've made their bed, and now they have to lie in it. I also said in my first book that it is our *sins* causing weather disasters on the earth, and not polluting or failing to recycle. I shared verses from Isaiah in order to prove my statement. I want to share them again in this book, because it is a message that California and many Americans still desperately need to hear today -

"THE EARTH IS DEFILED UNDER THE INHABITANTS THEREOF; BECAUSE THEY HAVE TRANSGRESSED THE LAWS, CHANGED THE ORDINANCE, BROKEN THE EVERLASTING COVENANT. THEREFORE HATH THE CURSE DEVOURED THE EARTH, AND THEY THAT DWELL THEREIN ARE DESOLATE: THEREFORE THE INHABITANTS OF THE EARTH ARE BURNED, AND FEW MEN LEFT." - ISAIAH 24:5-6

Until Californians learn to repent of their Godless ways, their State will continue to burn year after year. The majority of them have long defiled the earth with their sins. They have brought a curse upon their land, and have forgotten the God of our fathers - through whom all blessings flow. Thus, the recent headlines were correct in describing California resembling "Hell on Earth." It is God's Word coming to pass before our eyes. As Californians live like hellions, God will turn their State into a living *Hell* (Psalms 9:17). Unfortunately, Cali is far from alone. Many States across this nation are awaiting the judgment of God if they do not repent and return to Him soon. America, it is high time to return to your God. REPENT and return to the LORD... before it's too late.

I WILL PUNISH YOU ACCORDING TO THE FRUIT OF YOUR DOINGS, SAITH THE LORD: AND KINDLE A FIRE IN THE FOREST THEREOF... IT SHALL DEVOUR ALL THINGS ROUND ABOUT IT.

- JEREMIAH 21:14

CHAPTER SIX

PESTILENCES

JESUS SAID, THERE SHALL BE... PESTILENCES.

- MATTHEW 24:7 & LUKE 21:11

IN RECENT YEARS, HEALTH experts from numerous countries have issued warnings that the human race is at a greater risk of experiencing a global pandemic than ever before. They also warn that we're currently ill-prepared to combat a worldwide outbreak. Experts are in agreement, across the board, that it is not a matter of *if* a pandemic will strike but a matter of *when*. An infectious outbreak of SARS, cholera, bird flu, swine flu, Ebola, bioterror, or a brand new disease altogether, could kill millions. During the 2014-2016 Ebola epidemic, around 30,000 people were infected and one-third of them died from the disease.

We're at greater risk of witnessing a worldwide plague than any other time in history due to numerous factors - global travel, growing population, immigration, weather, and terrorism (just to name a few). The fact that the population of the U.S. had grown by leaps and bounds during the Obama years, due to an influx of refugees from the Middle East, means the possibility of a national pandemic has greatly increased. The immigrants pouring in from disease-prone Syria, and Mexico, are prime candidates for being carriers that will bring the next pandemic to America.

It is believed that, within 30 years, nearly 70% of the world's population will live in urban areas rather than less populated rural areas. In cities, interacting with thousands who could possibly be infected increases the chance of contracting disease. City-life also greatly increases the chance for disease to spread quickly, through something as simple as a touch, a cough, a kiss, or a bite. While many of the coming deadly diseases will most likely not originate in the USA, the easiest way they can arrive here is through global travel. Countries like Africa, or Middle East war zones like Syria, are breeding grounds for deadly diseases. An outbreak that begins on the other side of the globe will eventually make its way *here*.

That is exactly what happened with the Ebola pandemic. The disease, which spread rapidly in foreign nations, was undetectable for a few days. So, Americans traveling home from infected areas did not know that they had contracted the disease until they were back on U.S. soil. Luckily, the infected were quarantined and the deadly disease didn't spread as much as it could have. Experts say infectious agents can live in humans during the incubation period - which is the time between infection and the onset of symptoms. This means travelers can transmit an infection to another country before any onset of appearance of sickness. Billions of travelers crisscross the globe annually.

The SARS (Severe Acute Respiratory Syndrome) pandemic of 2003 began with Dr. Liu Jianlun, who developed symptoms of the airborne virus on a trip to China and then went to visit his family in Hong Kong. It is believed that he infected people at his hotel, along with family. In less than 4 months, nearly 4,000 cases and 550 deaths from SARS were traced to Liu's Hong Kong visit. More than 8,000 people became infected and nearly 800 had died, in more than 30 countries worldwide, because of just *one man*.

The country to country infections can also be spread through insects and animals. Travelers in airports became infected with malaria through mosquitoes that hitched rides on planes. In 2004, bird flu had crossed borders when Thai eagles were being traded as pets. A year earlier, Guinea rats that were carrying monkeypox were shipped as pets into America. 2009's H1N1 outbreak began in Mexico, and originated from pigs. That pandemic infected over 60-million Americans, and killed around 12,000. Nearly 600,000 had ultimately died from the disease globally.

Another big threat is bioterror. A genetically engineered virus is easier to make than a suicide bomb, and it could kill far more people than any bomb, gun, or even a nuclear weapon. ISIS and Al-Qaeda, who are both terror groups desiring the downfall of the USA, have made clear their intentions to use bioterrorism against the United States. Instead of suicide vests or running into military complexes with guns-a-blazing, a terrorist could easily weaponize a disease for a suicide bioterror attack - by exposing themself to a virus. All that they would have to do is enter a crowded airport, subway, arena, or heavily populated building, and touch any and everyone they possibly could.

This form of terrorism would kill far more people than any suicide bomb attack, as the perpetrator would claim more victims after the disease is spread. This has got to be one of the most disturbing scenarios of a global pandemic that I can think of. Yet, sadly, it's the most probable. A U.S. Naval War College professor, Captain Al Shimkus, told *Forbes*, "If ISIS ever wanted to send half a dozen of their operatives into an Ebola outbreak region, and intentionally expose themselves to the virus, they very well could. The idea is that once they intentionally infect themselves, they'd try to interact with as many people in their target city of choice." ISIS leaders say their fighters are willing to sacrifice themselves by spreading the Ebola virus.

A bipartisan Congressional report accused the administration of former President George W. Bush of doing too little to address the threat of bioterror. And during Barack Obama's presidency, a Congressional panel gave his government an "F" in preparedness.

Sources from the U.S. Border Patrol revealed that their agents had detained at least a dozen ISIS fighters at the U.S.-Mexican border during the Obama years.

Another factor that contributes to the risk of an outbreak is weather. Flooding events, in particular, greatly increase chances for waterborne diseases such as cholera, and for disease vectors like mosquitoes. With mosquitoes increasingly able to live in new unprotected territories, outbreak risk is high. With recent flooding from hurricanes like Harvey, Florence, and Michael, there could be numerous diseases spreading across the country as we speak. Mosquitoes brought Zika virus to America. In 2017, they carried it into over 125 cities in California. The Public Health Division of Communicable Disease Control laboratory-confirmed 530 cases of Zika infections in the State.

The experts agree that an uncontrolled pandemic or bioterror attack could result in the deaths of about 30-million people. They say that if another outbreak of a deadly disease were to occur, the nations of the world are "grossly unprepared." Now, I know this may all sound frightening and is very scary to ponder; but even if a global pandemic were to occur, there is one sure way to keep yourself and your family safe - FAITH. Even if this whole nation and world experience a plague unrivaled in history, believers can take heart that the LORD will keep us far from it. Read Psalms 91:3 - "Surely He shall deliver you from the noisome pestilence," and 91:6 - "We shall not fear pestilence that walks in darkness."

I like to think back to Exodus, and God's promise to "pass over" His people when the plagues came upon Egypt. Believers today have been living in a modern-day Egypt or Babylon, and I believe the LORD's age-old promises still ring just as true for His children today as they did for Jews. Though, instead of marking the doorposts of our homes with the blood of a lamb, we can now symbolically cover our doorposts and homes in the Blood of the *Lamb of God* - Christ Jesus. If God passed over His people when they had marked their homes in the blood of a mere animal, how much more will He now pass over us when we mark our homes in the holiest blood ever poured out on Planet Earth… the Blood of His only begotten Son?

I personally mark my home in the Blood of Jesus on every Passover feast, and He has kept His Biblical promise to keep the destroyer, the spoiler, plagues, disasters, and every evil, far away from my home. He will do the same for you when you dedicate your home to Him, mark it in the Blood of His Son, and believe *by faith*. There is no global plague that can ever claim the life of a believer if we put our trust in God's Word, repent of our sins, and diligently seek Him in times of national or personal distress. Here are some of the Biblical verses that I take heart in -

"AND THE BLOOD (OF THE LAMB) SHALL BE TO YOU FOR A TOKEN UPON THE HOUSES WHERE YE ARE: AND WHEN I SEE THE BLOOD, I WILL PASS OVER YOU, AND THE PLAGUE SHALL NOT BE UPON YOU TO DESTROY YOU, WHEN I SMITE THE LAND OF EGYPT, SAITH THE LORD." - EXODUS 12:13

"IF THOU WILT DILIGENTLY HEARKEN TO THE VOICE OF THE LORD THY GOD, AND WILT DO THAT WHICH IS RIGHT IN HIS SIGHT, AND WILT GIVE EAR TO HIS COMMANDMENTS, AND KEEP ALL HIS STATUTES, I WILL PUT NONE OF THESE DISEASES UPON THEE, WHICH I HAVE BROUGHT UPON THE EGYPTIANS: FOR I AM THE LORD THAT HEALETH THEE." - EXODUS 15:26

"YE SHALL SERVE THE LORD YOUR GOD, AND HE SHALL BLESS THY BREAD, AND THY WATER; AND I WILL TAKE SICKNESS AWAY FROM THE MIDST OF THEE." - EXODUS 23:25

"THE LORD WILL TAKE AWAY FROM THEE ALL SICKNESS, AND WILL PUT NONE OF THE EVIL DISEASES OF EGYPT, WHICH THOU KNOWEST, UPON THEE." - DEUTERONOMY 7:15

"HE WAS WOUNDED FOR OUR TRANSGRESSIONS, HE WAS BRUISED FOR OUR INIQUITIES: THE CHASTISEMENT OF OUR PEACE WAS UPON HIM; AND WITH HIS STRIPES WE ARE HEALED." - ISAIAH 53:5

"UNTO YOU THAT FEAR MY NAME SHALL THE SUN OF RIGHTEOUSNESS ARISE WITH HEALING IN HIS WINGS; AND YE SHALL GO FORTH, AND GROW UP AS CALVES OF THE STALL." - MALACHI 4:2

"THE PRAYER OF FAITH SHALL SAVE THE SICK; AND THE LORD SHALL RAISE HIM UP." - JAMES 5:15

"WHO HIS OWN SELF (JESUS CHRIST) BARE OUR SINS IN HIS OWN BODY ON THE TREE, THAT WE, BEING DEAD TO SINS, SHOULD LIVE UNTO RIGHTEOUSNESS: BY WHOSE STRIPES YE WERE HEALED." - 1ST PETER 2:24

Lord Jesus told us that, in the season of His imminent return, there would be *pestilences*. We have seen them popping up more and more over the course of the past decade, and I suspect they'll only grow worse leading up to His Second Coming. Thank God that true Bible believers will be raptured before the plagues of the Book of Revelation befall the heathen on Earth.

With so many other "Last Days" signs occurring around us in this generation, I am convinced that a national pandemic or global outbreak could begin any day now in the very near future. Since most people in this world are falling away from the Biblical Faith, fear and panic will grip many across the globe. While most of the secular world will seek out every vaccine under the sun to protect themselves from plagues, believers must follow the prescriptions given unto us by our Heavenly Physician. He has said that if we want to live healthy and safe in this world, and stay healthy and safe, then we need to...

- Have faith.

- Love the LORD with all of our hearts, souls, and minds.

- Keep His Commandments.

- Repent of our sins.

- Get washed and covered in the Blood of Jesus Christ.

- Pray without ceasing.

- Trust in the LORD.

Whether it be a physical or spiritual illness, there is no better medicine in the world for all that ails the human race than faith in God. If you don't have it, then you would be wise to FIND IT.

I LOOKED, AND BEHOLD A PALE HORSE: AND HIS NAME THAT SAT ON HIM WAS DEATH, AND HELL FOLLOWED WITH HIM. AND POWER WAS GIVEN UNTO THEM OVER THE FOURTH PART OF THE EARTH, TO KILL WITH SWORD, AND WITH HUNGER, AND WITH DEATH, AND WITH THE BEASTS OF THE EARTH.

- REVELATION 6:8

2020 UPDATE

CORONAVIRUS PANDEMIC

LESS THAN A YEAR after I had published this book, the world experienced much of what I had written about in this chapter. I'm not a prophet. I just believe every prophecy of the Bible, and that is why I feel the Holy Spirit led me to write these books - because the LORD needs someone to alert the world to what is coming on the horizon. The question you all need to ask yourselves is... if I was right about the global pandemic, prophesied in the Gospels about 2,000 years ago, then *what else* could I be right about?

America (and virtually every other country of the world) was on lockdown for months during Coronavirus (COVID-19). It felt like living out an End Times film about the Apocalypse. Actually, many who don't read the Bible believed it *was* the Apocalypse. It was not. It was just one of many pestilences that Lord Jesus said would come in the days leading up to the Rapture and His return. As I predicted in this chapter, the virus began on the other side of the world (China) and had made its way into America and the rest of the world through global travel. As I also predicted, it sparked great fear in unbelievers - hopefully leading to their salvation!

The pandemic left over a million dead globally, with 20% of the deaths in America, and about 40-million were infected around the world. Many have called it a once-in-a-lifetime event; but I'm sorry to say that my Holy Bible says THEY ARE WRONG.

CHAPTER SEVEN

WARS AND RUMOURS OF WARS

JESUS SAID, YE SHALL HEAR OF WARS AND RUMOURS OF
WARS: SEE THAT YE BE NOT TROUBLED: FOR ALL THESE
THINGS MUST COME TO PASS, BUT THE END IS NOT YET.

- MATTHEW 24:6/MARK 13:17/LUKE 21:9

THERE ARE MANY UNBELIEVERS who mock Bible Prophecy. One of the things you will hear them say most often is that "there have *always* been wars." While there most certainly have been, going back all the way to the days of Abraham (if not earlier), the wars which Jesus prophesied could only take place after 1948. As I explained in great detail in my first book, that all-important year started the clock on the season of the Rapture. '48 was the year of the biggest prophecy fulfillment since Christ left the earth nearly 2,000 years ago - the rebirth of the Nation of Israel. Without the Jewish State present on the world scene, none of the Holy Bible's "Last Days" prophecies could ever be fulfilled. A reborn Israel is absolutely central to Jesus coming back. It's where He returns!

Not to mention, after He defeats AntiChrist and Satan (who come against Israel) in the end, it is the Jewish State's Capital of Jerusalem where He will rule and reign from! In a nutshell, what all of this means is that every single war prior to '48 could not be a sign of the End Times. That includes World Wars 1 and 2. They meant nothing concerning Christ's return, but World War 3 will. It will be the war to end all wars, and is known to Bible believers as the Battle of Armageddon. The war will be staged in Megiddo in Israel's Jezreel Valley. Virtually all nations of this world will come against God's chosen Nation. When all hope seems lost for Israel, and destruction seems imminent, that's when their Messiah will make His long-awaited return. He will destroy their enemies.

Of course, their Messiah is our Lord Jesus Christ; and the war will be the culmination of the seven-year Tribulation on the earth. It is the AntiChrist who leads the charge against the Jewish State. Being Satan incarnate, he actually attempts to fight against Jesus - but is swiftly defeated and cast into "the lake of fire" (Revelation 19). Bible-believing Christians won't be here for the seven-year Tribulation, and will be raptured long before Armageddon begins. I believe the wars that Jesus referred to in Matthew 24, Mark 13, and Luke 21, are all wars post-1948 - especially the future Psalm 83 and Gog-Magog wars. The Psalm 83 battle is obviously found in Psalm 83, while Gog-Magog is described in Ezekiel 38-39.

Both wars, like the Battle of Armageddon, are the attempts by ungodly nations of the world to obliterate the Nation of Israel. We read in Psalm 83, verses 4-5, "They have said, Come, and let us cut them off from being a nation; that the name of Israel may be no more in remembrance. For they have consulted together with one consent: they are confederate against you." The last phrase refers to all of the Islamic nations that are mentioned in the Psalm forming a confederacy to make war on the Jewish State; and this confederacy will resemble the group of nations that came against Israel in the Six-Day War of 1967. Though, in the Psalm 83 War, the Arab nations that border and surround Israel will be joined by virtually *all* Islamic nations in the Middle East and Africa.

Just like in 1967, the Bible tells us that they will fail and that Israel will have another miraculous military victory. I suspect the defeat of the Muslim armies will lead to those nations crying out to Russia, who is allied with Israel's enemies in the Middle East, and this will lead to the Gog-Magog War. I'd written a good deal about the war in my previous book, so I refer you to the "Enemies of Israel" chapter in *The Signs of Our Times* if you haven't read it already. It'll give you a better knowledge of the war going further. Since I don't want to repeat all I had covered in the first book, I will just touch on a few key points about the war for anyone who has not yet read it.

I explained why "Gog" is the leader of Russia, and "Magog" is derived from "Magogites," who dwelt in what is today Russia. I connected the other names that were found in Ezekiel's prophecy - "Meshech, Tubal, and Rosh" - to Russia as well. This is why it is undeniable that the world's largest nation will someday lead the second largest war against the Nation of Israel. Who knows, if the AntiChrist comes from Russia, the Eurasian superpower may lead the Battle of Armageddon too. Believers will be raptured before the AntiChrist reveals himself, so all we can do is speculate about who it could be. I do believe he is alive and waiting in the wings.

In the first book, I also pointed out how Russia is currently closely allied with the *exact* nations that Ezekiel had prophesied it would be. Specifically, Iran (Persia) and Turkey (Togarmah) are two of Russia's closest allies on the world stage today. Ezekiel names them as the two closest confederates of Russia. His nearly 3,000-year-old prophecy is being fulfilled before our very eyes to a tee. Gog-Magog is fought on "the mountains of Israel," which would most likely be on the border of Syria in the Golan Heights region. It is beyond interesting to note that, as we speak, Russia has military boots on the ground in the Golan Heights to protect their interests in Syria.

It is not far-fetched to think that a flare-up between the IDF (Israel Defense Forces) and the Syrian army could claim lives of Russians stationed in the area. That could provoke Vladimir Putin of Russia to consider military action against Israel. Russia's made numerous public threats against Israel over the course of the past decade, leading me to believe that the Gog-Magog War is at the doors. In 2012, Russia had warned that an Israeli attack on Tehran (Iran's Capital) would be an attack on Moscow (Russia's Capital). The threat implied that any war between the Israelis and Iranians would lead to the Russians fighting alongside Iran, just as Ezekiel prophesied they would. It's no secret that Turkey's President hates Israel, so it is easy to envision the Turks joining forces with them.

Putin has allied Russia with virtually all of Israel's enemies. He has sent an abundance of high-powered weaponry to Iran and has held joint military exercises with them. Military protection of Syria's brutal dictator, by Russia, hasn't just caused deadly chaos in the country and Middle East region as a whole, but is in direct opposition to Israeli and U.S. forces on the ground and in the air. Russia is fighting alongside the Iranians in Syria's Civil War. The Israelis recently discovered that Russia placed surface-to-surface ballistic missiles in northern Syria. Two SS-26 Iskander missiles are vehicle-mounted, with launchers capable of carrying nuclear warheads with a range of 300 miles. Israel is only 50 miles away.

Given all the facts on the ground, it is impossible to deny that the wick of the powderkeg has been lit that could explode into the Gog-Magog War. Vladimir Putin is always itching to go to war. His regime possesses the most nuclear weapons in the world - even more than the USA. In 2017, Russia had about 2,000 nuclear warheads deployed. It is estimated that the superpower possesses about 4,400 of them today!

The U.S. is allied with Israel, and Russia with the enemies of the Jewish State. So, it's inevitable that America will see war with Russia in the not too distant future. In 2017, Putin was "furious" when America's President, Donald Trump, gave the order for two U.S. Navy Destroyers to bombard and destroy a Syrian air base with about 60 Tomahawk cruise missiles. The strike had been in response to the Assad regime's chemical weapons attack in NW

Syria, which left dozens of civilians dead. Not long after, a former Russian Defense Ministry spokesman revealed that Russia buried nuclear bombs off the coasts of America. Colonel Viktor Baranetz said the "mole nukes" would be used to trigger a tsunami which could drown major U.S. cities.

He explained that "While Americans deploy tanks, airplanes, and special forces battalions along Russia's border, we are quietly seeding the U.S. shoreline with nuclear mole missiles... They dig themselves into the ocean floor, and they will sleep until given the command to detonate... Oh, it seems I've said too much, I should hold my tongue." Baranetz claimed that no computer technology can pinpoint the location or calculate the trajectory of the Russian nuclear warheads. If his claims are true, then major U.S. cities - such as New York, Boston, and Miami - could be devastated by a historic tsunami when the nuclear bombs are detonated.

He said the bombs are aligned in a chain to cause a "massive tidal wave" when they are detonated together. Some of America's most populated coastal cities have been described as sitting ducks in the event of such an unconventional attack. The Foreign Policy experts believe that Russia will employ numerous methods of war against the United States before ever engaging in all-out nuclear war. Their current methods include cyber-attacks, EMP attacks, and "nuclear tsunami" option. Russian ships have been spotted off of America's coasts for years.

Iran, especially during the Obama administration, had parked warships off the U.S. East Coast many times. I wrote a lot about Iran, and their hatred for Israel, in the previous book. So, as with Russia, I do not want to repeat too much of what I already wrote. Please make sure that you read *The Signs of Our Times* to get all of the vital information that has led me to believe we are truly the Rapture generation. In 2017, a senior commander of the Iranian Revolutionary Guards said, "Over one hundred thousand missiles located all across the Middle East are ready to strike Israel at a moment's notice."

The leaders of Iran have long called for the destruction of the Jewish State - from their Supreme Leader to the President, and right on down the line. They all desire for Israel to be "wiped off of the map." In a 2018 video of the Islamic Revolutionary Guard Corps' military drills, the soldiers chanted "Death to Israel" and "Death to America," as a depiction of the White House and the Star of David were both split by a sword.

Besides Russia and Iran, the Israelis could much sooner see war with Hamas terrorists in Palestine's Gaza Strip and Hezbollah terrorists in Lebanon. In the 2014 war with Hamas, 5,000 rockets were fired into Israel. In 2006's war with Hezbollah, the terrorists launched 4,000 of them into the Jewish State. For more about the many threats that Israel has faced, is facing, and will face in the future, read the first book.

Finally, I can't write about *rumours of wars* and not mention North Korea. As of the publication of this book, the dictator of the country, Kim Jong-Un, has actually been playing nice. Since his 2018 Summit with U.S. President Trump, many believe he is genuine in his pledge to destroy his nuclear weapons in exchange for peace and security for his country. Given the history of North Korea, and their leaders, I am not buying it. With how much of a threat that NK has posed throughout the past few decades, you'd think they'd be mentioned in the Bible. By name, they are not. That is because there was no nation known by that name in the times when the Bible was written. Though, North Korea could be alluded to, along with China, in the Book of Revelation.

In Chapter 16, verse 13, we read "the kings of the east" - though some translations read "kings of the rising sun." I suspect this verse is specifically referring to China - the most powerful oriental nation. They're closely aligned with Russia and Iran in a Eurasian Union. It is likely that the verse is also referring to other

Asian nations, as it says "kings" (plural). If it does mean more than one Asian nation, then North Korea is undoubtedly a prime candidate. After all, China's long been one of the few allies that North Korea has had in this world. It is also hard to imagine a nuclear war without the trigger-happy NK regime being involved.

If the current nuclear talks with Kim Jong-Un and the United States were to break down, there is no doubt that he would return to his old threatening ways. Before the Summit with Trump, the leader said that his country was on the "brink of war." Depending on whether or not North Korea actually keeps their promises to destroy their nuclear arsenal (which I doubt), they are currently estimated to possess at least eight nuclear weapons. For years, Americans laughed at Kim Jong Un's failed missile launches; but in 2017, as his missiles began to fly much higher - much farther - and for much longer - we began to take the threat more seriously. Missile experts say that Kim's missiles were coming dangerously close to putting major U.S. cities within their range.

North Korea's ICBMs (Intercontinental Ballistic Missiles) were already capable of reaching the states of Alaska, Hawaii, and possibly even California. Some experts were going so far as to say that America's most populated cities, like Boston, Chicago, Denver, Los Angeles, and New York were *already* within range of Kim's missiles. In 2017 alone, North Korea launched 14 missiles - equivalent to 2 missiles per month. Besides the threat of nuclear attack, America faces an even greater possibility of falling victim to an EMP attack by North Korea, Iran, Russia, or China.

An EMP (Electromagnetic Pulse) attack could fry America's power grid, leaving one-quarter to one-half of the United States in total darkness, and it would put us back into the Stone Age. An EMP is a burst of electromagnetic energy, most known for being emitted from the Sun. It can now be man-made. EMP warfare is not as devastating as a nuclear attack initially, but it proves to be just as deadly over time and much harder to defend against. NK currently has two satellites orbiting over the U.S. that are capable of performing a surprise EMP attack at an altitude and trajectory that evades National Missile Defenses.

National Security expert, Peter Vincent Pry, has warned that North Korean satellites can be commanded to either deorbit to hit a target on the ground or explode at a high altitude. Both options would create an EMP effect, knocking out our power grid and the critical infrastructures that depend on it. By exploding a nuclear warhead in space, within 300 miles above any major city in the USA, a blackout of much of the nation's power grid would ensue after the blast mingles with the magnetic field. I'm sure that you will all be very comforted to know (sarcasm intended), though the Obama administration was put on high alert to this threat, the grid has been "defenseless" against such an attack. A powerful Solar Flare from the Sun or terror attack could fry our power grid.

Thankfully, Trump's administration has taken the threat more seriously. Still, there is much action that needs to be taken by the government to be able to defend against such a catastrophe. North Korean satellites are now orbiting at an altitude of 300 miles, with trajectories that put them daily over America. At this altitude, an EMP could impact much of the continental U.S., according to the EMP experts. Late last year, it was reported by the *Washington Examiner* that North Korea is not planning to give up all of its nuclear arsenal. Sources close to the Communist regime revealed that there are plans in place to use the weapons in the future to launch EMP attacks against their enemies.

We all take electricity for granted in today's day and age. Our cell phones, television, heating, air conditioning, and refrigerators would all be *useless* after an EMP attack. That's why the experts say it is the "biggest existential threat that our civilization faces." Homeland Security warns an attack on our power grid is coming, and it's not a matter of *if,* but *when.* A Commission of Congress that assesses the threat has said that such an attack could wipe out about 90% of the population within just two years of the event as a result of disease, food scarcity, and the complete breakdown of society. How inconvenient is it when we lose electricity for a day or two? Think of being without it for months to years!

While it may be scary to some to think that the "Last Days" wars which Jesus prophesied are on the horizon, the good news is that *His return* is on the horizon too! So, keep looking up.

THUS SAITH THE LORD GOD, THOU (GOG) SHALT COME FROM THY PLACE OUT OF THE NORTH PARTS, THOU, AND MANY PEOPLE WITH THEE, ALL OF THEM RIDING UPON HORSES, A GREAT COMPANY, AND A MIGHTY ARMY: AND THOU SHALT COME UP AGAINST MY PEOPLE OF ISRAEL, AS A CLOUD TO COVER THE LAND; IT SHALL BE IN THE LATTER DAYS.

- EZEKIEL 38:15-16

CHAPTER EIGHT

"2ND TIMOTHY 3" GENERATION

THIS KNOW ALSO, THAT IN THE LAST DAYS PERILOUS TIMES
SHALL COME. FOR MEN SHALL BE LOVERS OF THEIR OWN
SELVES, COVETOUS, BOASTERS, PROUD, BLASPHEMERS,
DISOBEDIENT TO PARENTS, UNTHANKFUL, UNHOLY,
WITHOUT NATURAL AFFECTION, TRUCEBREAKERS, FALSE
ACCUSERS, INCONTINENT, FIERCE, DESPISERS OF THOSE THAT
ARE GOOD, TRAITORS, HEADY, HIGHMINDED, LOVERS OF
PLEASURES MORE THAN LOVERS OF GOD; HAVING A FORM OF
GODLINESS, BUT DENYING THE POWER THEREOF: FROM SUCH
TURN AWAY... YEA, AND ALL THAT WILL LIVE GODLY IN
CHRIST JESUS SHALL SUFFER PERSECUTION.

- 2ND TIMOTHY 3:1-5 & 12

WHEN IT COMES TO signs of the Rapture and imminent return of Lord Jesus, there are certain Books and Chapters of the Holy Bible that always come to mind. Matthew 24, Luke 21, Mark 13, Revelation, Daniel, Ezekiel, and Joel, top the list of any Prophecy enthusiast. But one of the most thorough and detailed Chapters about the "Last Days" is actually found in a very unlikely place - within the letters of Saint Paul.

Paul's Epistles are widely regarded as the foundation for our Christian theology and ethics. His teachings reinforce or expand upon the teachings of Lord Jesus, and help us to blossom into the believers that God wants us to be. If you are part of a church that doesn't preach the Old Testament, chances are that a majority of your pastor's sermons or Bible studies are about Paul's life and teachings from the Books of Acts and Romans. Most pastors who teach solely from Acts and the writings of Paul, choosing to omit the rest of the Bible, do so because they don't care about Biblical Prophecy. They want to teach how you can be a better Christian *today*, and are not concerned with Christ coming back *tomorrow*.

Today, far too many of them are flat-out refusing to teach on the subject of End Times Prophecy. They either do not believe it themselves, or don't think their congregants will. As I pointed out in my previous book, they will say and do just about anything - or exclude just about everything - in order to keep the seats in their Megachurches filled. If only these worldly pastors knew that the same Paul, whose teachings they preach to steer clear of Biblical Prophecy, had actually started the doctrine of the Rapture!

He wrote extensively about the Last Days, in detail, and they would know that if they'd ever read past Acts and Romans. Paul revealed "the mystery" of the Rapture, which would precede the Tribulation and Second Coming, in 1st Corinthians 15:51-53 and in 1st Thessalonians 4:16-17. In both letters to Timothy, Paul laid out specific signs that would be occurring in the Last Days - in 1st Timothy, Chapter 4, and in 2nd Timothy, Chapter 3. In the latter, he gave (by my count) 22 unique signs. That is even more signs than Jesus gave in Matthew 24. So, do you think Paul wanted us to be preaching the return of the Lord? You betcha!

Those 22 signs of 2nd Timothy 3 are what this chapter will focus on - to prove, beyond a shadow of a doubt, that we are *the generation* which Paul had spoken of. I will tie each of them, one by one, to our society today. First, Paul warned that **"in the Last Days perilous times shall come."** The word "perilous" means dangerous. Have we been living in *dangerous* times? As I pointed out in *The Signs of Our Times*, global terrorism recently reached an all-time high. Mass shootings have become commonplace in our society. Day by day, regimes across the globe are building up nuclear arsenals. Each and every new year, it appears that World War 3 becomes a much greater possibility.

Due to reasons I had mentioned in the "Pestilences" chapter, disease outbreaks are now more possible than ever before. Some of the most powerful earthquakes in history have rattled the world in our generation. Hurricanes are bigger, stronger, and last much longer. And because of this society pushing our God out, immoral men and women are caring less and less for fellow human beings. Violence and rioting have become *cool* to kids of today. There is no one who can argue that our generation has not been living in very dangerous times. Paul also prophesied that men would be...

- **Lovers of their own selves** - Look around, turn on your television, watch any modern Hollywood or Music Award Show, follow the top athletes in any popular sport, or play any Hip Hop album out there today... and in every single instance, you'll find nothing but *vanity*. "You're the best" is what most of today's popular celebrities, athletes, and musicians long to hear. There is no humility found in the mainstream, except with famous Christians. Still, some of them let fame go to their heads. Virtually everyone wants to be hip and trendy today.

    They want others to love them for just *how great* they are. They desire the most followers or the most likes on social media, the most praise and glory, and biggest fan base that they can get. They crave your daily affirmation as a constant reminder of why they are *better than* you. They believe they *deserve* your adulation. It is somehow owed to them, because they were "born a star" and feel they should be treated like one.

Unlike them, true Christians do not care about any of that. We live humbly, putting the needs of others above our own. We don't need a lot of followers, but instead are leading others to follow Jesus. We don't care much about being liked, and we are more than happy with being hated for preaching the Word of God. We reserve all praise and glory solely for the LORD, and never for another human being - especially never for ourself! Sadly, there does not seem to be many of us *true* Christians left out there.

Today's Godless society tells you to "love yourself." They have got it all wrong. First and foremost, we are to love God - then our family - and then others. We don't need to love ourselves. We just need to be thankful and comforted by the fact that God loves us, and so it should not matter one bit what anyone else thinks of us. When you love God, family, and your neighbor, above yourself, everything else falls into place. When you love yourself first, everything else *falls apart.*

- **Covetous -** We are, no doubt, living in a generation that loves to "Keep up with the Joneses." Everyone seems to want what their neighbors have. Our society tells us that - in order to be cool - you must drive the newest models of cars, wear the trendiest clothes, possess the most recent phones or gadgets, and that you must have what everyone else around you has, or else you won't fit in. Even some Christians have forgotten that one of the Commandments is, "Thou shalt not covet *anything* that belongs to your neighbor." Modern believers have a big problem in trying to bring the outside world into the Church, as opposed to bringing the Church out to the sinful world.

It's hard to tell, in this generation, who is a Christian and who is not. Most everyone walks, talks, and acts the exact same. There are now even "Christian" rappers and heavy metal groups, because they seem to covet what the world outside of the Church has to offer. Honestly, aside from Johnny Cash, I'd agree with a lot of you that some Gospel music is plain boring. Though, that's no excuse to bring Satan's worldly music into God's House. What may be "boring" to this world will keep you *holy*. When you bring headbanging, twerking, or hip hop into any church, you leave the door wide open for the devil to enter in.

Yet, we wonder why many young believers are far from God in this generation. It is because they have made the world *their god*, instead of making God *their world*. Also, the LORD is clear that coveting does not just entail material possessions or wanting to be like the world. He specifically commands us to not covet the spouse of our neighbor. With the rapid rise of internet dating sites and apps, it's hard to find a marriage today without a cheater in it. Sadly, that even goes for Christian marriages.

With the growing ease of being able to quench lust at our fingertips, and the ability to talk to attractive strangers discreetly or even set up secret meetings with them over the internet, Satan is tempting every soul that he possibly can. The devil is having a field day destroying marriages today; and it's all due to *covetousness* - the sin of desiring and pursuing that which you cannot have. Remember one thing, brothers and sisters - Jesus said that if we *even look* upon someone else's spouse with lust in our hearts, then we've already committed adultery with them in our hearts (Matthew 5:28). I'd advise you to heed Paul's warning in James 1:14-15 -

"EVERY MAN IS TEMPTED, WHEN HE IS DRAWN AWAY OF HIS OWN LUST, AND ENTICED. THEN WHEN LUST

HATH CONCEIVED, IT BRINGETH FORTH SIN: AND SIN, WHEN IT IS FINISHED, BRINGETH FORTH DEATH."

What is the solution to this dilemma, plaguing many weak believers, in this culture laden with enticing sexual imagery and temptation around every corner? The Spirit of God. In Romans 8:6, we read that "The mind governed by *the flesh* is death, but the mind governed by *the Spirit* is life and peace." In Galatians 5:16, Paul encourages us to "Walk in the Spirit, and you shall not fulfil the lust of the flesh." When you truly know God and His Spirit and truly walk in the Spirit, you'll covet no more. You'll still struggle and be tempted. No one is immune to that in this carnal flesh. It is the devil's job, and he is not sleeping on it. He even tempted Jesus!

You can be sure that he'll try you when opportunity presents itself. The next time that he does, how will you respond? Will you fold like an accordion, giving in to the lust and temptation, without putting up any fight? Or will you respond like Jesus did, and rebuke him with the Word of God? Submit yourself to the LORD. Resist the devil, and he will flee from you! (James 4:7) Stand strong, and take heart in 1st Corinthians 10:13 -

"THERE HAS NO TEMPTATION TAKEN YOU BUT SUCH AS IS COMMON TO MAN: BUT GOD IS FAITHFUL, WHO WILL NOT ALLOW YOU TO BE TEMPTED ABOVE THAT YOU ARE ABLE; BUT WILL WITH THE TEMPTATION ALSO MAKE A WAY TO ESCAPE, THAT YOU MAY BE ABLE TO BEAR IT."

Obviously, the moral of the story is to *stop coveting*! God will provide for our every need, and every good gift is from above. So, don't desire the worldly things that are here today and gone tomorrow; but set your heart on the things that last for eternity. Thank God for the blessings that you already have, such as family, pets, roof over your head, transportation, food, drink, and the clothes on your body. If you covet anything, covet His blessings!

- **Boasters -** I am sure you have heard the song, "Anything you can do, I can do better - I can do anything better than you." That seems to be the theme song of this generation. It seems no one wants to build others up these days, only tear down - so that *self* can be exalted. A majority of this generation, especially celebrities and those in the public eye, desire to be the absolute best at what they do. Now, if they were doing that for the right reasons, such as to honour God or to help others, that would be praiseworthy. Sadly, most do not. They only do it to be braggadocious. This generation is chock-full of *boasters*.

- **Proud -** Another thing that our generation is filled with is *pride*. I penned an entire chapter about the "pride" of the LGBT community in my previous book. Their pride is no different than that of Lucifer. Pride is rebellion against the LORD and His Will. To be proud is to be self-centered and to take great pleasure in a certain aspect of your life - whether looks, accomplishments, or lifestyle. Your way is the right way, and you could care less what others have to say or for what God thinks. The LGBTQ movement is a perfect example of the pride of the devil, because in their proud attitude they actually *celebrate* their sin.

    They are more than happy to rebel against Almighty God, because they feel that they're right and He's wrong. A lot of them are well aware that His Word says the way they are living is morally wrong, but they just don't care.

As long as it makes them feel good, the opinion of their Creator takes a back seat. It is all about *them*, and only them. They remind me of Lucifer with his five "I"s. We read in Isaiah 14:12-14, he said, "I will... I will... I will... I will... I will..." He was so puffed up in his pride that he even said he would "be like" God. The LORD rebuked him, and said, no... "you will be brought down to Hell." We all know how things turned out for old Lucifer.

God is saying the exact same thing through His Word to all those who follow in the footsteps of Lucifer today - in their pride, they will be brought down to Hell. There is no escaping that fate until they repent, and turn from their wicked ways and their open rebellion against the LORD.

- **Blasphemers** - I've written an entire chapter of this book on blasphemy, because it's become so widespread in our generation. You will read all about it soon.

- **Disobedient to parents** - Growing up, if my brother or I were to act up and disobey our parents, my father would always dish out the discipline. It was through the lashes to our backside from his belt, or by being grounded time and time again, that we'd both learned right from wrong. In today's generation, children are little hellions. It has to be their way, right away, or else they will throw a temper tantrum. Kids actually physically strike or fight with their parents. This was unheard of a decade ago. I have heard many kids raise their voices to their parents, or even cuss at them in public. It is unbelievable.

This generation is the first to see children be blatantly disobedient to their parents, without question. This "Last Days" prophecy has only been fulfilled in *our day*. A big reason behind the downright demonic behavior of today's youngsters is twofold - parents wanting to be their child's *friend* instead of authority, and not raising them to fear God. If children are raised in a Christian home, then they should be learning God's Word. If they were, then they'd know the Fifth Commandment - "Honor your father and your mother." The youth are so disrespectful because they are not being reared according to Proverbs 22:6.

Another verse from the Book of Proverbs, in Chapter 13 and verse 24, says if you spare the rod (modern belt) from a child, who needs discipline, then you *hate* them. Think about that... In God's eyes, if you do not chastise your son or daughter for doing wrong, then you do not love them. Why should He be concerned about blessing your children if you don't love them yourself?

Many parents today are afraid to discipline their kids because their children threaten to call the cops or Child Protective Services. I guarantee you, 9 times out of 10, if a police officer shows up at your home and you tell him you spanked your kid for disrespecting you, or for doing something bad, the officer would tell the child not to call again because they got what they had coming. Obviously, Biblical discipline does not entail beating or abusing your child. That is not what I'm talking about. I'm saying that God's just fine with you using that belt around your waist to teach your child respect.

When I was younger, I despised my Dad for it. Your kids will probably say they hate you for it too. But the more that my father spared not the rod, the more lessons I learned. I learned to fear him and his authority. Because of that, I grew up to fear God and His Authority. If your children do not fear their earthly father and mother, then how can they be expected to fear their Father in Heaven? If they dishonour you, they'll grow up to dishonour Him.

I'm forever grateful I had received discipline as a child. If I didn't, then none of you would be reading this book. I would not have become the man that I am today. So show these rebellious kids who's boss, and spare not the rod!

- **Unthankful** - There are many today who would say that this generation is not unthankful. They most likely point to everyone giving thanks on Thanksgiving Day and most always to their family, friends, or to someone who does something nice for them. The "unthankful" that Paul was prophesying meant being unthankful to GOD. When was the last time that you've seen #ThanksBeToGod trending on social media? Sadly, I never have. On Thanksgiving, a national holiday created by our founders for us all to give thanks to the LORD for His countless blessings upon our nation, this generation gives thanks to everyone *but Him.*

  I have had arguments with atheists over Thanksgiving many a time, as they try to say that it is a secular holiday having absolutely nothing to do with God. My response to them is always, "Well then *who* are you *thankful to* for your blessings?" Their answer is that they can be thankful to others *without* being thankful to God. No. You cannot. It is so unbelievable. It is *GOD* Who gives rain upon the heads of the righteous and wicked alike. He alone blesses every human being on Earth. If someone does something nice for you, to enhance your life in some way, it is the LORD Who orchestrates that. If someone does something evil to you, then it is the *other guy* inspiring that (Satan).

  The fact is *all* that is good comes from God. There's nothing good that does not proceed from Him. Too many people today will thank other people all day long, but will never give God His due thanks, praise, and glory. I see it all too often. This generation wants their blessings but, at the same time, wants nothing to do with God Who gives them. It's so sad. Next Thanksgiving, I want you to take a look at everyone posting on social media what they are thankful for, and who they are thankful to, and count how many of them mention the LORD. My guess is that you'll be able to count them all on one hand. God forgive this unthankful generation.

- **Unholy** - Is this the most unholy generation since Jesus Christ ascended into Heaven around 2,000 years ago? I'd say that it is. There seems to be no reverence for God or His holy things anymore. Churches are being shut down, boarded up, and bulldozed, more than ever in the history of America. People don't want to hear about living *holy* these days. It's a drag to them. There's just too much fun found in sin. For those who desire to, how are we to live holy in the first place? By observing the Commandments of our all-Holy God.

    Now, obviously, we cannot keep them all; but we are called to at least strive to. Lord Jesus said that we should try to be holy and perfect, just as our Father in Heaven is Holy and Perfect. How many around you, even Christians today, do you see striving to be holy? I, for one, only see a lot of in-name-only Christians - becoming more *worldly* as opposed to more holy. I will touch on so many unholy things being said and done all around us in the chapters, "Demonic Indoctrination" and "Widespread Blasphemy." The worst and most unholy thing that I have witnessed in our generation is irreverence toward the Word of God.

    I wrote in my first book about how I leave boxes of Holy Bibles out in public places for anyone to freely take. Unfortunately, I've found that not only do a lot of people want nothing to do with God or His Word, but some are downright hostile and hateful toward it. Believe it or not, as I couldn't believe it myself, some people have actually *desecrated* the Bibles. They've torn pages and soaked the Bibles in damaging liquids, like milk, mustard, and ranch dressing. I couldn't believe my eyes. It's simply demonic to do that to the Holiest Book in the history of mankind. It bothers me that people like that are actually living in the same neighborhood.

If people can do that to the Bible, then *what else* are they capable of doing? Or should I say... *not* capable of doing? It's one thing if you do not believe in God, but it is a whole 'nother thing to be downright hostile toward your Creator and spit on His Word. I wish that I could say that it was just one lost soul who was possessed by the devil; but, unfortunately, the desecration has been done by more than one person in multiple locations.

Ten years ago, if someone was caught intentionally defiling the Holy Bible in any way, they would rightfully be excommunicated from town. They'd be the one who was spit on, and would be shunned. They'd accurately be called sick, twisted, disgusting, and evil. Today, because of the utter lack of respect for God's Word, most people will just shake their heads and keep walking. There is no righteous indignation anymore. Our society's become the epitome of *unholy*.

- **Without natural affection** - Historically, there have been two ways this has been interpreted. **1:** Men and women would lack the God-given natural feeling to love others - even family. According to a Scottish Theologian, William Barclay, some people considered children a misfortune in the days of Paul. He said that when a child was born, the child was taken and laid at the father's feet. If the father lifted up the child, it meant that he acknowledged it. If he turned away and left it on the ground, then the child was thrown out - *literally*. There was not a night that went by when 40 abandoned children were not left in the Roman forum. Babies born weakly or deformed were drowned.

Can we make modern-day connections to this lack of respect for life? Sadly, we can. The abortion-on-demand plaguing our society is just like the heartless murder of babies in the days of Paul. Instead of the father literally having a baby laid at his feet and walking away from it, some dads today refuse to take responsibility for children after impregnating the mother. They say that they do not want the "burden" of having to father a child.

There are also mothers today, who consider the baby to be a burden, who turn to the organizations like Planned Parenthood to help them murder the child before it's even born. There are horrific stories of unwanted babies being left inside of dumpsters or on street corners today, just as they were left abandoned in the streets of Paul's days. We are no doubt seeing this prophecy of 2nd Timothy 3 being played out before our eyes *every day* in this generation.

2: Some have also interpreted this prophecy of Paul to mean not having affection for others in the natural way that God ordained us to from the beginning. This would be referring to homosexuals and pedophiles. The natural plan for affection was to be between a man and woman. The two love each other spiritually and physically, enter into a marriage union, and then produce children. This is the natural order. Paul explained in Romans (Chapter 1), and God laid it out clearly in the Old Testament as well, that those lying with the same sex are living unnaturally. The LORD called this type of affection "abomination" in Leviticus 18:22.

Do we see this version of the prophecy being fulfilled in our day and age? Homosexuality is more common than ever before in our nation's history, and same-sex marriage is now legal and widely accepted across this country. I'd go so far as to say that unnatural sexual lifestyles are even more prevalent in our generation than they have ever been in world history, since the days of Sodom and Gomorrah. Either way you interpret Paul's prophecy, both meanings of "without natural affection" are being fulfilled today.

- **Trucebreakers** - When we hear the word "truce," most think of an agreement made between two parties that are engaged in battle to stop fighting. The word had a much deeper meaning in the days of Paul. A trucebreaker, more often than not, was someone who had broken a covenant. Reading the prophecy of Paul in that light, just how many covenant-breakers do we have in this generation? As far as those who have broken covenant with God, the answer would be: too many to count.

How about those who have broken the covenant of marriage? According to a CDC report, titled "100 Years of Divorce and Marriage Statistics," divorce statistics had not been recorded prior to 1867. So, starting with the late 1800's as our starting point, have there been more or less divorces over the course of the past 150 years? I think we all know the answer to that question.

Between the years 1867-1900, the divorce rate started at .03% and rose to .07% during the period of 30+ years. By 1930, it had risen to .16%. By 1940, .19%. In 1950, it reached .26%. Up until 1967, it pretty much stayed the same and even dropped a bit from year to year. In 1970, things changed dramatically for the worse, as the divorce rate had jumped to .35%. Throughout the 70's, it climbed every year. By 1979, it skyrocketed to .53%. Thankfully, that was the peak decade for divorces in our generation - but not for good reason. The divorce rate had fluctuated between .40 and .53% up until the year 2000.

The reasoning given for the rising trend ending was more women using birth control and less young people getting married in the first place. Both of these things go against God's Will for the human race. In the year 2000, there were about 1-million divorces. Since that time, up until today, there have been between 800,000 to just over 950,000 divorces every year. While you'd think it would be a positive thing that divorces per year had fallen from over 2-million just 50 years ago to under 1-million today, remember it's because less people are getting married.

A recent study, conducted by the Institute for Family Studies, showed that less than 50% of adults in the U.S. between the ages of 18-64 are married. And, according to census data, this marks an *all-time low* in America. So, at the end of the day, we see how this generation has been filled with "covenant-breakers"; and we can also see how, most recently, many want absolutely *nothing at all* to do with covenants. Either way is displeasing to our Creator.

- **False accusers -** In today's day and age, if you are a Holy Bible-thumping Christian like me, you are all too familiar with false accusers. We're called "haters" or "bigots," our words twisted, and lies are spread about us far and wide. In Matthew 5:11, Jesus prophesied this would happen to His followers in the Latter-Days. Today, we see someone accused of doing vile things all of the time. Whether the target is a President or Supreme Court Justice, there is a Godless crowd who'll do anything to silence adversaries and further agendas. The false accusers are all around us.

- **Incontinent** - The Biblical definition of this word is "not being able to restrain lusts or appetites, particularly of the flesh." It can also mean "unchaste or lewd." I often refer to today's younger generation as the "Tinder generation." Young people aren't looking for husbands or wives. They are only looking for mates with whom they can satisfy their sexual needs. I've mentioned that the marriage rate in America is at an all-time low, and that's because young people do not want spouses, families, or kids; they simply want "friends with benefits."

  Now, of course, sex is wonderful when it is enjoyed within God's boundaries - "on a marriage bed undefiled" (Hebrews 13:4). But sex outside of marriage makes you a "whoremonger" or an "adulterer" in God's sight. Think about it... in the eyes of the LORD, our generation is full of whoremongers and adulterers. Sadly, this society that needs Jesus more than ever has pushed Him further away than ever. With the rise of the internet, pornography has been easier than ever to access. Children stumble across sex-laden websites with little to no effort, often by simply misspelling a search term or a site address. Incontinence has truly *engulfed our continent.*

- **Fierce** - In the Holy Bible, "fierce" is defined as violent, threatening, cruel, savage, and even murderous. I've lived on this earth for 38 years, and I can never remember a time when the hearts of men have been so cold. Are men today *violent*? These days, protests are not protests - they are violent riots. Boxing gloves are considered too tame for our society, so men are now obsessed with maiming each other in MMA fighting. The more blood and broken bones, the more the crowds go crazy for it.

Are men *threatening* today? I once again point to this generation's obsession with violent rioting in order to get their way. When radicals want something today, they will threaten you until they get what it is that they desire. It is all too common in our day and age.

Are men *cruel* today? Just how many times have you heard the phrase, "it's a cruel world"? You have probably heard it a lot, because it is true. Most people seem to only be concerned about themselves and *their* needs; so they will step on and hurt others, for any reason, in the process of getting whatever they want. There are too many who are used and abused by cruel human beings, and there is also the abhorrent abuse of animals in our world. As a pet owner, I get sick to my stomach when I hear of animal cruelty and torture.

Are men more *savage* and *murderous* today than they were in past generations? Read the "Terrorism" chapter in my previous book, and you've already read the chapter on "Mass Shootings" in this book, to find that the answer to this question is a resounding YES.

- **Despisers of those that are good** - In Chapter 15 of the Gospel of John, Lord Jesus said that we would be "hated" for following Him and believing the Holy Bible. He said this evil world would hate us for holding to God's Law in the midst of a society that's laden with sin. Jesus exposed the sins of the world, and made us all aware that we need a Saviour. People who love sin don't wanna hear that. So, they hated Him. Now, they hate us. They persecuted Him. Now, they are persecuting us. Bible believers who live to please the LORD, keep His Commandments, and do the things that He says are good, are despised with a passion.

The more sinful this world becomes, the more we are looked upon as the dregs of society. We're reviled all day long. For what exactly? Do we physically harm anyone, or treat people wrong? Absolutely not. We are despised simply for believing and preaching God's Word of truth in this world filled with Satan's lies. Our Godless society fulfills Isaiah 5:20, which says, "evil will be called good and good evil." Just turn on your television... Things that God calls evil, perverted, and abominable, are celebrated as "good" things. Meanwhile, most things that the LORD says are good are despised as "evil" - along with those of us who espouse such things.

- **Traitors -** This is someone who betrays family, friends, or country. Judas Iscariot is the poster child for traitors. Traitors care about no one but themselves, and will betray anyone to save their own hides or obtain reward. Treason has been, in all ages, regarded as one of the worst crimes that a man can commit. How much betrayal do we see in the Church alone? Pastors and priests have been turning their backs on Christ and God's Word, so that they can be friends of this world. How many betrayals are we seeing in relationships today? How many cheat on their spouses or significant others? The answer to these questions is, without a doubt, *far too many* to count.

- **Heady -** Being heady means you are "self-willed." Your way is better than everyone else's way, even better than God's Will for your life. Many in this generation seem to think that they know better than the LORD. His ways are no longer acceptable to them. The liberal thinkers of this day and age feel that the God's Word is outdated, and that it needs to be revised to better suit modern society. They think they're so wise, and many follow after their Godless ideologies. They need to read 1st Corinthians 3:18-20 -

"IF ANY MAN AMONG YOU SEEMS TO BE WISE IN THIS WORLD, LET HIM BECOME A FOOL, THAT HE MAY BE WISE. THE WISDOM OF THIS WORLD IS FOOLISHNESS WITH GOD. IT IS WRITTEN, HE TAKES THE WISE IN THEIR OWN CRAFTINESS. AND, THE LORD KNOWS THE THOUGHTS OF THE WISE, THAT THEY ARE VAIN."

- **Highminded** - This word goes hand in hand with "lovers of their own selves, boasters, the proud, and the heady."

- **Lovers of pleasures more than lovers of God** - In the Greek, the word that translates to "lovers of pleasures" in our Holy Bible is "philodonos." This word is a compound of two words - "phileo" and "hedonos." Phileo conveys love and affection. The word "hedonism" actually stems from hedonos. Hedonism is the pursuit of pleasure, and sensual self indulgence. If you're a hedonist, then you're addicted to doing or obtaining anything that brings you personal pleasure. You don't care if what you do or want is right or wrong. If it makes you feel good, you will do anything to obtain what it is that you desire.

  So, Paul was prophesying that, in the Last Days, men and women would be obsessed and consumed with what brings them pleasure - as opposed to them doing what is pleasing to our LORD. This generation has drifted further away from God than any other that has come before us; because we have been inundated with far more things to preoccupy our minds and senses, and keep someone from devoting time to God's Word. While television, radio, and the internet can be good, when they're used for the right reasons - especially to build up your faith or the faith of others - these things can also pull you away from God, and can *keep you away*.

The devil uses all tools at his disposal, even if they were not originally designed to hamper our walk with the LORD. He'll use TV, music, the internet, phones, social media, video games, and more. One of the tools that he's used most successfully to damage your faith and life, in the name of pleasure, is pornography. The addiction to pornography is a disease infecting the hearts and minds of billions of people around the globe, even Christians. Porn can forever alter spiritual growth of the youth, cause men to view women as objects, and inspires the crime of rape. In the U.S., there've been between 200,000-400,000 sexual assaults per year throughout the past decade.

There are so many things that people turn to today for pleasure and happiness, all the while forgetting that the best happiness and serenity can be found in God alone. When you love the pleasures of the world more than you love the LORD, you'll never truly be happy. Never. You can have brief moments of satisfaction, but they will not last very long. Only the joy and peace that Christ Jesus brings us, from the Father, truly lasts - and lasts forever.

Modern research can prove this Biblical message that I'm preaching. Even with far more toys and gadgets than ever before to bring us all pleasure today, the "Worldwide Happiness Index" is the lowest on record. Whenever you pursue happiness through anything other than God, and His Word, it will elude you. So, put the Holy Bible at the forefront of your life, and you'll find happiness and peace in everything that you do. I guarantee it.

- **Having a form of Godliness, but denying the power thereof -** Paul is speaking of Christians who *say* that they believe in God, but who *live* like the unbelieving world. How many of those do we see among us? Read the last two chapters of *The Signs of Our Times*, and you will find that the answer is: more than are not. Today, too many in-name-only Christians either complain that the LORD doesn't answer prayers, are entertaining other "religions," or are departing from the Faith altogether. The reason that they aren't finding fulfillment in the Faith is because they are not utilizing the power thereof.

They are not praying without ceasing. They are not believing every aspect of the Word. They are not studying the Holy Bible as diligently as they should. They are not following God's Laws. They are not truly believing - by faith - everything that God has said and promised. While being professing-Christians, they may appear "Godly" to others in the secular world; but they will never be able to obtain or realize the power that God's Word brings - as long as they are living *like* the secular world.

As I've said before, too many Christian leaders and modern churches are concerned with bringing *the world* into the Church, when they should be striving to bring *the Church* out to the world! Until the day that they do, they will be Godly *in-name-only* - but that is all.

- **Suffering persecution for being Christian -** This is one prophecy of Paul that's been fulfilled more so than at any other time in history, since the days that he penned it. Go back and read the "Christian Persecution" chapter of my previous book, and the first chapter of this book. We are, no doubt, that "hated by all" generation of Christians that Lord Jesus prophesied would come "in the Last Days."

- **Evil men and seducers will wax worse and worse, deceiving, and being deceived** - "Evil" is defined as any thought, attitude, or action, that is contrary to the Will of God. It's best understood as the polar opposite of "good." We all know *God is good.* That is because He is caring, faithful, holy, just, loving, merciful, and the embodiment of truth. His Laws are wholly moral. On the flipside, it is no secret that Satan's evil. He's deceiving, selfish, unholy, corrupt, hateful, cruel, and the father of lies. His ways are wholly immoral.

How many today share the aforementioned qualities of the devil? Also, how many exemplify qualities of the LORD among us? I'd think anyone with a working moral compass has to admit that more men follow after Satan, than are being imitators of God (Ephesians 5:1). Whether atheists, antichrists, anti-Semites, animal abusers, rapists, murderers, or flat-out Satanists, they all wax worse by the day. Plus, New Age gurus deceive others with unBiblical nonsense; while they're being deceived *themselves* by the demons posing as *angels of light* (2nd Corinthians 11:14).

As for the seducers... Most always in the Bible, the word "seduce" means "lead astray". In verse 13, seducers means "impostors." These men are better known in our day and age as false prophets. I am going to need a whole lot more paper to address them, so the coming chapter will be all about this final sign of 2nd Timothy 3.

EVIL MEN AND SEDUCERS SHALL WAX WORSE AND WORSE,
DECEIVING, AND BEING DECEIVED.

- 2ND TIMOTHY 3:13

CHAPTER NINE

FALSE PROPHETS

JESUS SAID, MANY FALSE PROPHETS SHALL RISE, AND SHALL
DECEIVE MANY... INSOMUCH THAT, IF IT WERE POSSIBLE,
THEY SHALL DECEIVE THE VERY ELECT (BELIEVERS).

- MATTHEW 24:11 & 24

WHEN SAINT PAUL REFERRED to "seducers" in 2nd Timothy
3:13, I believe that he meant "fake Christians." There is definitely
no shortage of them in our generation. These are they who stand
in front of the pulpit preaching their *own* ideas about what God
wants for us - as opposed to what His Word actually says. Many
pastors today get their theological degrees, but do not personally
know the LORD. Thus, they preach messages which are any and
everything *but* Biblical. The great preacher, Jack Van Impe, best
described the false prophets of our day and age as having "a head
knowledge of God, but no *heart* knowledge."

So-called pastors and priests, even the Pope, preach self-help
sermons, get-rich quick messages, or are pushing liberal agendas
- all under the banner of Christ. Satan is loving every minute of it,
as he employs counterfeit Christian leaders to drive souls away
from eternal truth and into comfortable falsehoods. Today, instead
of the Church being all about God and what He *did* for our souls,
the prevailing message of many Christian "teachers" is that it's all

about you and what God can *do* for your wallet. Thus, instead of looking to the Cross for salvation, MegaChurch pastors have you looking to a divine money tree for satisfaction. These seducers are deceiving so many across the globe. At the same time, they themselves are being deceived by Satan.

Many of these pastors probably think that they are doing right by God, with their worldly prosperity preaching, and have no idea that Satan's sifting them (and their congregations) like wheat. The devil is not only leading so-called shepherds astray, but the flocks in the process. Far too many false prophets are in our world today, and come in many different forms. First of all, I want to address prosperity preachers, who are getting rich off believers struggling financially. The followers of these popular preachers are already behind on bills. Yet, they are told that the more they bless their pastor, the more they themselves will be blessed. These preachers teach that "The LORD wants you to be rich and prosperous," but apparently you can only attain your riches *after* enriching *them*.

Now, understand, I am all for tithing... just not to billionaire false prophets! Also, I take no pleasure in alienating or calling out other believers. I wish we were all united around the happy hope that Jesus is coming back soon. Still, at the same time, I cannot remain silent when I see many wolves in sheep's clothing robbing brothers and sisters in Christ blind. So, I intend to name names. First, I want to start with a name that even unbelievers across the world are familiar with: **Joel Osteen**. Joel has refused to preach on Bible Prophecy and the return of our Lord. He always dodges questions about social issues of our day, such as homosexuality or abortion, and that is how he's amassed 50,000 attendees per week at his church (Lakewood) in Houston, Texas.

He, like Rick Warren, knows that this backslidden generation doesn't want to hear about sin, and so he only preaches messages that *they* want to hear - not the message that *God* wants them to hear. His type of ministry reminds me of a verse from Isaiah. In

Chapter 30, verse 10, in which worldly sinners say to the men of God: "Prophesy *not* unto us right things, speak unto us smooth things, prophesy *deceits*." And another verse that comes to mind is 2nd Timothy 4:3 -

"FOR THE TIME WILL COME WHEN THEY WILL NOT ENDURE SOUND DOCTRINE; AFTER THEIR OWN LUSTS SHALL THEY HEAP TO THEMSELVES TEACHERS, HAVING ITCHING EARS."

"Sound doctrine" refers to God's Word - *all of it*. The LORD says that, in the Last Days, men and women of the world will no longer want to hear what He has to say about right and wrong. They will only want to hear about His blessings, and never His judgments for refusing to repent of their sins. So, Paul said that they'd be seeking out Christian "teachers" who'd tickle their ears with prosperity (lusts of the world) sermons. Osteen is at the top of that list. His preaching style is best summed up by the title of his best-selling book, *Your Best Life Now*. Let's break down the words of this title, and see how it does or doesn't line up with the Holy Bible, shall we?

YOUR... If you took your time reading the previous chapter then you would know that doctrines of self-gratification or selfish ambition are frowned upon by God. Jesus had laid out the selfless example we are to follow as believers. I previously explained that we are to love God *first*, then family, then others, and ourselves *last*. If we do this, then the LORD will take care of us. When you focus only on *your* needs and not on God, you'll always be *needy*.

The next word Osteen used to attract readers is **BEST**. Joel seems to think we should strive to accumulate as much wealth, material things, fame, and glory as we possibly can in this life. He teaches that you should desire the absolute *best* for yourself. This is opposed to what God's Word teaches about humbling yourself in this world, and seeking *His best* for your life. We should all be content with what we have, and with what the LORD provides for us. If God wants you to be financially rich, you will be. I, myself, am content with a roof over my head, a car to drive (even if it's over 20-years old), stocked cupboards and fridge, and in knowing my loved ones are in good health and alive and well. Everything else that I'll ever receive from the LORD is just an extra blessing.

In this wicked world, I don't expect to sell a million copies of my books like the Osteens of the world. I know preaching God's truth won't gain me a very large fanbase. Preaching what people want to hear, like Joel, most certainly would. I am called as God's prophets of old were, to preach His Word - in season and out of season, whether the people like it or they don't like it; correcting, rebuking, and encouraging with complete patience and *doctrine* (2nd Timothy 4:2). I do not seek fame, only Heavenly rewards for leading lost souls to God. Nor do I seek glory, but only to bring the LORD the glory that is due Him.

The third word that Osteen used is **LIFE**. He preaches that you should be focusing on *this* life, here and **NOW**. These final two words are the antithesis of what the LORD desires for us. We are not to focus on the temporal things of this life, but on eternal things (2nd Corinthians 4:18). We should be concerned only with our *eternal* lives and if we will be right with God in the hereafter - through Christ. We should not be concerned with enriching our *present* life, which can pull us away from God. This may be hard for a lot of people to hear; but I am now writing my second book, am not going hungry, have a healthy family, and I am not lacking anything I need in life. God provides for every need, and is giving me the *best days of my life now* because I am focused on *eternity.*

Again, I may never be a world-acclaimed Best-Selling author - but I know God is pleased with me, and that is all that should matter to a believer. Joel, on the other hand, needs his $10-million mansion and a $50-million net worth to validate his faith. Do you remember how big Lord Jesus' home was? Don't forget, He was God in the flesh. It just so happens, as an adult, Jesus didn't have a home! How about Saint Paul? Was he traveling from city to city in a golden chariot? No. The soles of his feet had been covered in calluses from traveling the Middle East and beyond in some beat up pair of sandals. The disciples all left their homes, families, and possessions, to follow Jesus. Were Paul and the disciples all living their "Best Lives Now"? Not by a longshot!

I know it may seem like I am singling out Osteen, but I most certainly am not. There are others preaching the same prosperity gospel that he does, and who are getting rich off the contributions of their congregations. **Jesse Duplantis** has said, "If Jesus were to descend from Heaven and physically set foot on 21st-century Earth, He would probably take a pass on riding on the back of a donkey... He'd be on an airplane preaching the gospel all over the world." Preaching the Gospel wasn't Jesus' job - it's ours. His job was finished at Calvary. Rest assured, Christ would not be flying on a golden Learjet if He were on Earth today (even though He is the King of kings and the Lord of lords).

Remember that Jesus humbled Himself as a servant, though He was the One who deserved to be served. He chose the donkey to ride into Jerusalem, showing the type of King that He was. He wasn't like worldly kings who are concerned with war and riches. No. He was the Prince of Peace, concerned with helping the poor and needy. Today, I guarantee you that Jesus would still be riding a donkey and certainly not driving a Mercedes Benz. The reason for Duplantis making the "donkey" statement was because he was asking his congregation for $54-million to help him buy a luxury jet to "spread the Gospel" around the world. The jet he desired was a Falcon 7x, which would be his ministry's 4th jet (all paid for by his followers' "offerings to God").

Another preacher in love with luxurious jets is **Creflo Dollar**. In 2015, he started "Project G650," which would be financed by his 200,000 followers. The project would fund the purchase of a $65-million Gulfstream G650 private jet for Dollar's "ministry."

Kenneth Copeland is another who used his ministry's donations to purchase a Gulfstream V jet, which cost tens of millions. After he acquired the plane, Copeland told his followers that it needed upgrades totalling $2.5-million. He said he needed a new hangar, maintenance equipment, and a longer runway to accommodate it.

Pastor **John Gray**, who rose to fame as the star of a reality TV show on Oprah Winfrey's OWN Network, once worked under Joel Osteen. So, his craving for worldly riches must run deep. He is now a Pastor of his own church in Greenville, South Carolina. Last year, Gray made the headlines after he purchased a $200,000 Lamborghini for his wife's anniversary gift. His excuse was that he is 45-years-old, and shouldn't have to wait until he is 70 to live his *best life*. Where have I heard *those* two words before?

The next dangerous teaching, and teacher, I need to address is "New Testament Only" Christianity and **Andy Stanley**. He is, by far, the most well-known pastor who advocates for Christians to "throw out" the Old Testament of our Holy Bible. In early 2019, he made headlines across Christian news outlets for saying that Christians need to "forget the Ten Commandments." Shame! Men like him *should* forget the Old Testament, because he obviously needs a lot more study of the New! He teaches that Jesus wants us to focus on *one* singular commandment: "love one another." Yet, *thousands* of words are attributed to our Lord in the Bible. If all He wanted us to remember was one phrase, then why did He tell the disciples and Paul to record everything else that He said?

If one commandment was all He came to teach us, then why would He have His followers write nearly 185,000 words, making up roughly 8,000 verses, in 260 Chapters? Sure seems to me that Jesus wanted us to learn and remember a whole lot more than just 3 words. It certainly appears that way, doesn't it? While "love one another as I have loved you" is an important teaching, and central to our Faith, we can't live by that command alone. According to Stanley's logic, Jesus doesn't care if we sin every second of every day - so long as we love one another. So, you can blaspheme the Spirit, worship false gods, take God's Name in vain, sleep with family, live as a prostitute or porn addict or pedophile, and the list could go on and on - so long as you simply "love one another."

Can you see how Stanley's view of the Holy Bible is flawed? Also, in advocating that we throw out the Old Testament, he is in total disagreement with Jesus Himself. As believers in the Triune God - Father, Son, and Holy Spirit - we believe that Jesus and the Father YHWH wrote the *entire* Bible together, through the Holy Spirit. So, Jesus actually wrote the Ten Commandments with the Father. Why then would He want His followers to "throw them out"? Answer: He wouldn't. He didn't. He actually commanded us to *keep them* in Matthew 19:17. Jesus said that there was a *greater* commandment than His command to "love one another." If Stanley actually studied the Bible that he supposedly preaches, then he would know that.

In Matthew 22, verses 37-38, Jesus said, "You shall love the Lord your God with all your heart, and with all your soul, and with all your mind." He said that this is not only the first, but the *great commandment*. When we love the LORD first, and obey His commands, we will "love one another." The heretical teaching of Stanley is not just theologically irresponsible, but also spiritually dangerous. He portrays Jesus, not as Holy Son of Almighty God - not as co-Creator of the Universe - not as Living God come down to dwell among His children - not as Saviour of mankind - but as a hippie who is simply all about "groovy peace and love."

Yes, Jesus Christ is love. God is love. You cannot know true love in this world unless you know our Father in Heaven and the Lord Jesus. But Jesus isn't some teacher like Gandhi or the Dalai Lama. He was, is, and forever will be *GOD*. He is King of kings and Lord of lords. So, He had a lot more to teach us poor sinners than just "love one another." Men like Stanley don't care though. They want to keep the seats filled in their churches. That is why they preach messages everyone on Earth can get on board with. Stanley currently has around 30,000 members of his Megachurch. Anyone else notice that the pastors who preach the *least* Biblical truth and doctrine always seem to have the most followers?

I have got a piece of advice for everyone... If you are seeking a church today that truly preaches the Word of God, look for the smallest building on the block with the smallest congregation. I guarantee they preach the truth, and their church is empty because nobody wants to hear it. Speaking of backslidden churches, that would bring me to **Rick Warren**. In the "Falling Away From the Faith" chapter of my first book, I addressed his "purpose-driven" plan for churches in great detail. I'd also highlighted other false prophets, like those promoting or endorsing sins of Gay Marriage, transgenderism, and abortion. Not to mention, those teaching the demonic doctrine that God is "gender-neutral" - as opposed to *the Male* He has portrayed Himself as throughout the *entire* Bible.

Someone else who I had mentioned in the previous book was **Pope Francis**. I constantly refer to him as the uber-liberal Pope. He's so far to the left, on so many issues, you would think he was a politician - rather than the leader of over one-billion Christians worldwide. In *The Signs of Our Times*, I pointed out just some of the blasphemous things he has said and done. In this book, I have selected the most heretical statements of Francis that I could find - to show why I believe him to be a false prophet. He has said...

- *"Many think differently, feel differently, seeking God or meeting God in different ways. In this crowd, and range of religions, there is only one certainty that we have for all: we are all children of God."*

- *"I belong to this religion, or that one. It doesn't matter!"*

Oh, it matters Francis. Our Holy Bible is clear that we are only "all children of God" *by faith in Christ Jesus* (Galatians 3:26). Anyone who is not washed clean of their sins by our Lord, and anyone who follows after false gods (Allah, Krishna, Buddha, etc.) - is *not* a child of God! They may be created by Him, as all human beings are, but they are *illegitimate* children.

- *"It is true that the idea of conquest is inherent in the soul of Islam. However, it is possible to interpret the objective in Matthew's Gospel, where Jesus sends his disciples to all nations, in terms of the same idea of conquest."*

- *"It is wrong to equate violence with the religion of Islam, and characterization of Islam as violent is untrue... If I speak of Islamic violence, I should also speak of Catholic violence. I believe that in pretty much every religion there is always a small group of fundamentalists."*

First off, Islamic conquest involves violence, terror, and war, as called for by Muhammad and Allah. Jesus' Great Commission to His disciples and to all future believers was in no way, shape, or form, the *same idea* of conquest. Those peacefully preaching the Gospel of God's grace and salvation to strangers across the globe is a polar opposite of Islamic invasion of non-Muslim lands and *forcing* the inhabitants of those lands to worship their god or die. Francis says "all religions have violent fundamentalists, and Islam is no more violent than Catholicism." Where on Earth did this man ever get his theological degree? Clown College?!

So many of his statements totally contradict the Holy Bible. How in the world can someone with such little knowledge of the Word of God be elected to lead an entire global denomination of the Faith? It is dangerous to have someone like him shepherding so many in the Lord's flock around the world. Francis needs to read chapter 3 of my previous book, where I point out the many differences between Islam and Judaism/Christianity. There is no possible way that the two Gods could be the same. I listed verses from the Quran to prove my point. Whether politically correct or not, and whether Francis likes to admit it or not, Islam is the most violent and deadly "religion" on the face of the planet. It has been since its inception.

- *"We all love Mother Earth, because she is the one who has given us life and safeguards us."*

There is no "Mother Earth" - only a "Father in Heaven." It is HE Who has given us life and safeguards us. As the Pope, Francis should know this basic fact of the Faith. You would think.

- *"When we read about Creation in Genesis, we can run the risk of imagining God was a magician, with a magic wand able to do everything, but that is not so."*

- *"Evolution is not inconsistent with a notion of Creation."*

The LORD was absolutely able to do everything in Creation! Not because "He's a magician with a magic wand," but because He is GOD! And, as I also explained in the first book, evolution is 100% inconsistent with the notion of Creation. Living things did not evolve. They were *created*. If you don't believe that, then you just don't believe God's Word. I, for one, will forever believe the LORD over mentally ill men like Charles Darwin.

- *"There is no Hell."*

The reason why I refer to Francis as the "uber-liberal" Pope is because he so very often sacrifices Biblical doctrine at the altar of political correctness. Of course, most people do not want to hear about everlasting torment in unquenchable fire - where there will be weeping and gnashing of teeth. It is a scary thought. The fact is that Hell is *just as real* of a place as Heaven. If there were no Hell, then Jesus Christ came and laid down His life for nothing. His sacrifice would be meaningless. If we are all going to Heaven at the end of the road, and there is no punishment for sins against our Holy God and Father, then why would He have suffered and died to keep us from an *imaginary* place of eternal torment?

Jesus was with the Father YHWH "in the beginning" (John 1:1). He was there when everything was created, seen and unseen. In fact, Hebrews 1:2 tells us that it was "through Lord Jesus" that God created "the worlds" (Universe). So, Jesus did what He did for us because He knew *for a fact* that Hell was all too real. The good news of Christ is that not one human being on this earth has to go there if we would just put our faith and hope in Him. His precious shed Blood cleanses us of *all* sin. All that you and I have to do is repent, and do our utmost best to turn from our wicked ways. If there were such a thing as a "Get out of Hell free" card, it would bear an image of our Lord on the Cross!

If the Pope were to actually study the Holy Bible, which over one-billion Catholics on Earth expect him to represent, then he'd find that one Person had talked about Hell more than anyone else. Was it the Apostle Paul, as so many think? No. How about one of the Old Testament prophets, who spoke a great deal about God's judgment? Nope. Maybe Noah? Abraham? Moses? King David? The answer is no, on all counts. So then, Who spoke about Hell the most? The answer to the question might shock you. Believe it or not, it was Lord JESUS. He taught about Hell around 60 times in the New Testament. All the "many paths to Heaven" believers, who ignore "Hellfire and brimstone" preaching because they only believe Jesus' words, obviously need to study their Bibles!

I have compiled a few verses where our Lord had described the eternal reality of Hell -

"THE SON OF MAN SHALL SEND FORTH HIS ANGELS, AND THEY SHALL GATHER OUT OF HIS KINGDOM ALL THINGS THAT OFFEND, AND THEM WHICH DO INIQUITY; AND SHALL CAST THEM INTO A FURNACE OF FIRE: THERE SHALL BE WAILING AND GNASHING OF TEETH." - MATTHEW 13:41-42

"AND IF THY HAND OFFEND THEE, CUT IT OFF: IT IS BETTER FOR THEE TO ENTER INTO LIFE MAIMED, THAN HAVING TWO HANDS TO GO INTO HELL, INTO THE FIRE THAT NEVER SHALL BE QUENCHED: WHERE THEIR WORM DIETH NOT, AND THE FIRE IS NOT QUENCHED. AND IF THY FOOT OFFEND THEE, CUT IT OFF: IT IS BETTER FOR THEE TO ENTER HALT INTO LIFE, THAN HAVING TWO FEET TO BE CAST INTO HELL, INTO THE FIRE THAT NEVER SHALL BE QUENCHED: WHERE THEIR WORM DIETH NOT, AND THE FIRE IS NOT QUENCHED. AND IF THINE EYE OFFEND THEE, PLUCK IT OUT: IT IS BETTER FOR THEE TO ENTER INTO THE KINGDOM OF GOD WITH ONE EYE, THAN HAVING TWO EYES TO BE CAST INTO HELL FIRE." - MARK 9:43-47

"AND I SAY UNTO YOU MY FRIENDS, BE NOT AFRAID OF THEM THAT KILL THE BODY, AND AFTER THAT HAVE NO MORE THAT THEY CAN DO. BUT I WILL FOREWARN YOU WHOM YE SHALL FEAR: FEAR HIM, WHICH AFTER HE HATH KILLED HATH POWER TO CAST INTO HELL; YEA, I SAY UNTO YOU, FEAR HIM." - LUKE 12:4-5

"IF A MAN ABIDE NOT IN ME, HE IS CAST FORTH AS A BRANCH, AND IS WITHERED; AND MEN GATHER THEM, CAST THEM INTO THE FIRE, AND THEY ARE BURNED." - JOHN 15:6

"THE FEARFUL, AND UNBELIEVING, AND ABOMINABLE, AND MURDERERS, AND WHOREMONGERS, AND SORCERERS, AND IDOLATERS, AND LIARS, SHALL HAVE THEIR PART IN THE LAKE

Francis teaching that there is "no Hell" is in direct opposition to the words of Christ. It is also an extremely dangerous teaching. When people begin to believe that there is no eternal punishment for doing evil, then evil will most certainly increase. Francis has got to be the most Biblically-illiterate Pope in history. In my first book, I mentioned that he doesn't seem to care very much about God's love for the Nation of Israel. He was the first Pope to ever recognize and embrace a "State of Palestine." If he picked up the Bible sometime, he'd know that the LORD loves the Jewish State more than any other nation in all of history. By befriending the enemies of Israel, the Pope stands with the devil (1st Chronicles 21:1) - and not the God that he *claims to be* representing.

This Pope could be the False Prophet of Revelation (Chapter 13). The Christian *impostor* will hold a great authority over most believers on the earth, and will lead them astray from the truth to follow after AntiChrist. He'll establish and lead the "One World Religion." Given all of the statements of Francis that I've shared, it is obvious that he'd love to lead a religion that incorporates all faiths of the world into one global body. If you are a Catholic that follows after the Pope, or if you are an Evangelical who follows men like Osteen or Stanley, I'm not condemning you for teachers you have chosen to follow. I do, however, have a piece of advice for you - and I hope that you will take it...

If what your Pope, preacher, pastor, or priest, is teaching does not match up with what the Holy Bible says, then FORGET IT. It is not of God, and it is not worth remembering!

THERE WERE FALSE PROPHETS AMONG THE PEOPLE, EVEN AS THERE SHALL BE FALSE TEACHERS AMONG YOU, WHO PRIVILY SHALL BRING IN DAMNABLE HERESIES, EVEN DENYING THE LORD THAT BOUGHT THEM.

- 2ND PETER 2:1

CHAPTER TEN

DEMONIC INDOCTRINATION

NOW THE SPIRIT SPEAKETH EXPRESSLY, THAT IN THE LATTER
TIMES SOME SHALL DEPART FROM THE FAITH, GIVING HEED
TO SEDUCING SPIRITS, AND DOCTRINES OF DEVILS (DEMONS).

- 1ST TIMOTHY 4:1

MAINSTREAM MEDIA TODAY IS no doubt under the control of
Satan. Broadcast television has become nothing short of demonic.
In just the past few years, there have been popular TV series that
have been all about the devil himself. A majority of them actually
paint him in a good light. A FOX drama (now on Netflix) is titled
Lucifer, and it portrays Satan as a likable guy in human flesh. The
show's main character, Lucifer Morningstar, is supposed to make
the devil look "cool." He drives a fancy car, owns a nightclub in
L.A., and is irresistible to women. He is described as "a good guy
who is bored and unhappy as the keeper of Hell."

In the script, Satan resigns his throne, abandons his kingdom,
and "retires" to Los Angeles. God sends an angel to convince him
to return to the underworld. Morningstar questions the angel, "Do
you think I'm the devil because I'm inherently evil or because
dear old Dad decided I was?" This question is supposed to make
people rethink Biblical teachings about good and evil, and about
God and Satan. It is spiritually dangerous for viewers, especially

young people who don't know much about the Bible. A similar series, titled *Damien*, which had been cancelled by A&E after just one season, presented the Antichrist as another likable young guy who didn't seem that inherently evil.

Meanwhile, Lord Jesus and the Bible are being consistently blasphemed and mocked across network and cable television. On an episode of AMC's *Preacher*, the main character tore pages out of the Holy Bible to use them as rolling paper for smoking weed. The NBC comedy, *Superstore*, had deeply offended Christians by suggesting that Jesus "not only supported Gay Marriage," but that "HE was gay." I'll bet NBC would never say those things about Muhammad of Islam. A blasphemous Adult Swim series, called *Black Jesus*, portrays our Lord as a foul-mouthed, weed-smoking, liquor-drinking, gang-related African American man in Compton. Where is the outrage?!

What's worse, if that were possible, so-called Family-friendly networks are regularly promoting sinful trash to the youth. Disney has incorporated gay characters into popular series and cartoons; as well as in popular films, like 2017's remake of *Beauty and the Beast*. ABC Family went so far as to air the first-ever televised kiss between two underage boys. Netflix had recently rolled out a remake of the lighthearted sitcom *Sabrina the Teenage Witch*, and retitled it *The Chilling Adventures of Sabrina*. In a departure from the original, the revamped version is dubbed "extremely Satanic." It targets the same audience as its predecessor - teenage girls, but is filled with "plenty of blood and gore," and features demons.

America's youth are being subjected to far more sex, profane language, and violence, during traditional early-evening "family hours" of broadcast television viewing than ever before. There's a watchdog group, known as the Parents Television Council (PTC), that studied animated TV shows ranked highest among viewers aged 12-17. They monitored them for about a month, and viewed around 125 episodes. They found a total of nearly 1,500 incidents of explicit sex, drugs, and/or offensive language, within 57 hours of programming. Another study found sexual content rose nearly 25% from 2001 to 2007. That was just over ten years ago. I can only imagine what those numbers are like today.

Parents today must be especially vigilant in monitoring what their kids are watching, because long gone are the days of leaving them alone for hours in front of the tube. The devil wants all of our souls; and if he can't get yours, then he wants your children. He's using the media as his outlet to do that. If not TV or movies, he'll use music. Most popular musicians today have some type of demonic messaging in songs, videos, and performances. Whether it's Ariana Grande and her song "*God is a Woman*," Jay Z and his obsession with Occult symbolism, Beyonce's demonic rituals in live performances, Lil Uzi Vert - whose name is a nod to Lucifer, or Marilyn Manson tearing up the Bible, there is no shortage of Satanic indoctrination (even worship) going on in music today.

The devil has his hands all over the internet as well. Besides flooding the net with pornography, he's inspired the big three tech giants to be extremely hostile toward Bible believers. Read about the neverending suppression and censorship that I've endured on Facebook over the years on my website, *BiblicalSigns.com*. Also, Twitter was recently exposed for "shadowbanning" conservative Christians. And it has long been thought by Holy Bible believers that Google holds an anti-Christian bias. In early 2018, we found undeniable proof to confirm our suspicions.

Many Christians who used the smart device, Google Home, which is similar to Alexa from Amazon, recorded videos of what appeared to be a blatant omission of our Lord Jesus Christ by the programmers at Google. The virtual assistant voice in the Google Home device (and some smartphones) gave detailed biographies for every religious figure in the world, except for one... JESUS. Google could tell you all about Allah and Muhammad of Islam, Buddha, Krishna, and other false gods; but as for the Saviour of the world, God in the flesh, the King of kings, and Lord of lords, absolutely *nothing*. His Name is more well known than any other figure in history, and He is so important to mankind that we keep time by Him (BC and AD). Yet, Google has *no clue* who He is.

It was obvious censorship of "the Name above all names." In videos documenting Google's cluelessness when it came to Jesus, users had asked the device who some other religious figures were. In one viral video, a Google user asked who Allah was. She got a very long thorough response from the Google assistant. She went on to ask who Buddha, Krishna, and some other "gods" were. She received detailed profiles for every single one of them. Others had asked about Satan, Muhammad, or Joseph Smith of Mormonism, and also got long descriptions for them all. Yet, whenever Google Home or Google smartphones were asked about Jesus, the virtual assistant replied, "Sorry, I don't know how to help with that yet," or "My apologies. I don't understand."

Sadly, it was not the first time Google had been called out for appearing anti-Christian. 2018 marked the 18th year in a row that the Google company didn't recognize Easter in their main page's Google Doodle; and Christmas has only ever been represented by secular images like snowmen, toys, and Santa Claus. The Doodle is a graphic that displays the company name above the search tab on Google's website. The images commemorate special occasions and major holidays... *except* the ones that are Biblical apparently. Throughout Google's history, there have been Doodles for Islam's Ramadan, Hindu religious festivals, and even for LGBT Pride.

I recently read a study which found Google Search is biased in favor of left-wing and liberal domains, but against conservative and Christian sites, with a confidence of 95%. Well that explains a whole lot! I've attempted to submit my website as a News outlet to Google many times since its 2015 inception, and it is always rejected. Meanwhile, search Google News today and you will find sites littered with nothing but ads - or blogs with less than 10,000 visitors. You would think that never having to retract or correct an article, and having over 1-million visitors, makes my site worthy of inclusion into Google News; but obviously none of that matters to them. They don't want you hearing my *Biblical* point of view.

Google and the lamestream media don't want you to be a free thinker. They want you to think how *they* tell you to think. There is a whole lot of brainwashing going on in the media today, which is why we must always stay rooted in God's Word. The powers that be at Facebook, Twitter, Google, New York Times, HuffPost, Washington Post, CNN, NBC, PBS, and others in the mainstream media, aim *to shape* your worldview. The absolute last worldview that they want you to hold is one that is Bible-based. Since they can't stop you from picking up a Bible at home, or from attending church, they force-feed you beliefs and opinions that are contrary to your Faith. They're obviously dead set on reprogramming your minds to think like they do. Are you going to let them?

One man that they want you to hate is the current President. Now, I've never been a superfan of Donald J. Trump, but I do not dislike him either. Unlike most Americans, I've been pretty much neutral when it comes to the 45th President. He's done some fine things for Christians and for Israel, and for that he has earned my respect. I bring him up, because it is no secret that the lamestream media loathes him *with a passion.* Yet, the exact same "unbiased" media had praised Barack Obama. You never once saw a negative story about the former President ever air on CNN. Today, they're anti-Trump 24-7. It's often too nauseating to watch. It is not just Donald Trump who they hate though. It is also anyone who holds firmly to the traditional Biblical worldview.

They have demonized Christian role models like the patriarch of *Duck Dynasty,* Phil Robertson, as well as Tim Tebow, and the Benham Brothers. If I were more well known in the mainstream, be sure that I'd make headlines as an intolerant, closed-minded, homophobic, Islamophobic, Bible-thumping bigot and hater. That is why I rightly call the liberal media CHRISTIANOPHOBIC.

Given all that I've shared in this chapter, it is no wonder that Christianity's been on the decline in America throughout the past decade. What's even worse is that something has to fill the void. That explains why Satanism and Witchcraft are thriving in 2019. There are now more Americans who identify with Witchcraft than the entire Christian denomination of Presbyterians (1.5-million). In 2018, there were stories about witches across the U.S. placing hexes and curses on President Trump and Supreme Court Justice Brett Kavanaugh. One witch who led a hex against Kavanaugh, Dakota Bracciale, said that she was "absolutely willing to cause physical harm" through her witchcraft. She should be arrested!

The rise of Satan in this country is the reason that so many Godless liberals today want you *gone* if you dare to disagree with them. I've actually heard left-wingers say that Christians "need to die." Nothing, and no one, but the devil himself could inspire that kind of hatred toward another human being. Satanic temples are popping up all across the USA, and Satanic monuments are being displayed at State Capitols to protest our Nativity Scenes or Ten Commandments monuments. America is a fallen nation, and is in desperate need of revival more than ever before in history. If we Christians do not courageously stand up to these demonic spirits infiltrating our country, and corrupting the soul of America, then the USA may soon suffer the fate of Babylon the great.

THE ANGEL CRIED MIGHTILY WITH A STRONG VOICE, SAYING, BABYLON THE GREAT IS FALLEN, IS FALLEN, AND IS BECOME THE HABITATION OF DEVILS, AND THE HOLD OF EVERY FOUL SPIRIT, AND A CAGE OF EVERY UNCLEAN AND HATEFUL BIRD.

- REVELATION 18:2

CHAPTER ELEVEN

WIDESPREAD BLASPHEMY

IN THE LAST DAYS... MEN SHALL BE BLASPHEMERS.

- 2ND TIMOTHY 3:2

"THERE IS NO FEAR of God before their eyes." This verse, from Chapter 3 of Romans, has come to my mind too often throughout the course of the past decade. Whenever I think that the utter lack of respect for God cannot possibly get any worse, someone sets a new low. In *The Signs of Our Times*, I highlighted many cases of blasphemy. I found it necessary to pen a whole chapter on the sad subject in this book because of how common and widespread it's become. I don't think there's ever been a generation, since Jesus ascended into Heaven, that has ever been more irreverent toward our Creator. I'm beginning to think that the God-haters are trying to outdo each other, regarding how far some of them go to slander the Holiest Book on Earth.

Just last year, I read one of the most blasphemous things that I have ever heard in my life. Brian G. Murphy, a gay activist who actually calls himself a "Christian," is co-founder of the "Queer Theology" website. In a video that he made for the website, he'd claimed that Jesus is "polyamorous," and that believers should be too. "I'm Christian and I'm polyamorous. I'm also kind of a slut. A reclaimed empowering kind of a slut – *like Jesus*," he said. He went on to say, "If you're one of those Christians who believe in having a personal relationship with Jesus Christ, well He's having personal relationships with billions of other people. He's kind of a relationship slut." This ignoramus actually had the nerve to call the Saviour of the world a "slut"!

What's the world coming to when that kind of garbage being spewed about the Son of Almighty God has become acceptable? How can anyone, even with the wildest imagination, ever accuse the only Being in the history of mankind - who *never* sinned - of being a slut?! This confused soul can call himself a Christian all that he desires, but I guarantee that he is not and never will be - as long as he promotes such demonic lies from the pit of Hell.

He actually claims that the Book of Ephesians supports his "theology." He said, "In Ephesians 5, Paul uses the word marriage to refer to Jesus' relationship with us. Repeatedly, Paul reminds us that Jesus gave himself for us. Us... the Church - which Paul has described as the whole body of believers. In this marriage, He isn't married to one person. He's married to the entire body. He is in a pansexual, polyamorous relationship with us. So, Christians can be polyamorous. It is a Biblical model of relationships." This guy has obviously never thoroughly studied the Holy Bible. He is just another, in a long line of cherry-pickers, who takes verses out of context in order to support his perverted beliefs.

First off, Murphy says the Church is made up of all believers. On that statement, he is right; *but* what he conveniently failed to mention is that the Holy Bible always refers to Christ's Church in *female* terminology. Read what Paul says in the *same* Chapter that Murphy claims backs up his theology -

"HUSBANDS, LOVE YOUR WIVES, AS CHRIST LOVED THE CHURCH AND GAVE HIMSELF UP FOR HER, THAT HE MIGHT SANCTIFY HER, HAVING CLEANSED HER BY THE WASHING OF WATER WITH THE WORD." - EPHESIANS 5:25-26

Not only did the LORD inspire Paul to distinctly describe the Church with a female pronoun, but He made him repeat the word "her" *three times*! When God speaks, we are to listen attentively. When He repeats Himself, we must pay extra close attention. God made sure to liken the marriage of the Church unto Christ to the marriage between a *husband and wife*. So, NO Murphy, Jesus is not in a "polyamorous" relationship with the Church. He is most certainly not "pansexual" either. For those who don't know what that lingo means, it is defined as having a sexual attraction toward others "regardless of their sex or gender identity."

Factually, Jesus Christ was not, is not, and will never ever be attracted to men. Never - no matter how much some perverts in the LGBT community try to twist and pervert verses of the Holy Bible to make it appear so. He was and is the sinless Son of God. He was and is our Holy "God in the flesh." In Revelation 22:15, He mentions unrepentant homosexuals in a list of those who will not enter Heaven at the end of the road. So, how could He *engage* in homosexual relationships? He couldn't! He didn't! He won't! This nonsense really needs to stop. It ticks me off so much when homosexuals, so ignorant to the Bible's teachings, claim God says something that He most certainly has not and does not.

Yet, there's something that riles me up even more - when men from *inside* "the Church" teach abominable lies to other believers. Believe it or not, one such man recently blasphemed even *worse* than "Queer Theology" boy. I am speaking of a professor at the College of the Holy Cross in Massachusetts. In 2013, Tat-Siong Benny Liew was appointed as Chair of New Testament Studies at the university. Someone needs to pull the Chair out from under him! Because things that he teaches, in a Catholic school no less, I can't even print in this book. His words are much too vulgar and blasphemous. I'll do my best to convey the filth he's propagating to students, without using the same profane language that he has.

Liew has said that Jesus Christ is not just the King of Israel and King of the Jews, but that he's also a "DRAG KING"! What Liew's implying is that Lord Jesus was a crossdresser! This kind of heresy makes me sick to my stomach. I hate to even entertain his ridiculous belief, but I have to make sure that I teach the truth of what God's Word actually says. Christ Jesus, who was with the Father in the beginning, co-authored *every word* of the Holy Bible through the Holy Spirit (2nd Peter 1:21). Chapter 22, and verse 5, of Deuteronomy says -

"THE WOMAN SHALL NOT WEAR THAT WHICH PERTAINETH UNTO A MAN, NEITHER SHALL A MAN PUT ON A WOMAN'S GARMENT: FOR ALL THAT DO SO ARE ABOMINATION UNTO THE LORD THY GOD."

There is no way that Jesus would have ever crossdressed! He kept the Law of His Father perfectly while on the earth, living a totally sinless life to become an acceptable unblemished sacrifice on behalf of our sins. Liew's statement is ludicrous. While you'd think that there could not possibly be a more blasphemous claim any worse than that, Liew actually made quite a few more. He has said that, in the Gospel of John, there are many verses that show Jesus exhibited "homosexual tendencies." How in the world could a Christian school give this idiot the time of day? It is bad enough that he got the job as a teacher at the college, but it's even worse that he still holds the position of authority today - six years later!

In yet another preposterous statement, Liew said that John's constant references to Jesus "wanting, giving, and leaking water," spoke to "gender indeterminacy" - and that led to "cross-dressing and queer desires." Whaaaaaaat?! Liew's head is in a fantasy land far far away. How does anyone, in a right state of mind, concoct such perverted ideas while reading the Holiest Book on the earth? He is a pervert of the highest degree. Speaking such blasphemous drivel about the Lord of our souls should be illegal everywhere on

Earth. I don't want to go on writing about what else this so-called "professor" said about Christ but, sadly, I have to - to prove that this generation is unparalleled when it comes to blasphemy.

Liew has also said (as I try to prevent myself from vomiting) that "the episode of Jesus washing the disciples' feet at the Last Supper was suggestive... a literary striptease... even seductive... because it showed and withheld at the same time." Sick! This guy belongs working behind the counter of an Adult Video Store - not teaching at a Christian college! Finally, in statements that I cannot clean up enough to print in this book (they are words found only in pornographic material), he implies that Christ desired and *had* sexual relations with His disciples and (in the most blasphemous thing you will ever hear) even with our Father in Heaven! Okay, now I really have to puke. This guy has major issues.

Normally, right about now, I'd give all of the Biblical verses in which God condemns homosexual sex and incest; but I should definitely not have to do so in this instance. I'd hope every person on Planet Earth, believer or not, should know that our Holy God would not engage in "incestuous" relations with His Holy Son. If that is even remotely conceivable in your mind, then I don't want to know you. I don't ever want to live in a world so perverted. It pains me physically to have to write this garbage in my book, but I'm hoping it has gotten my point across that blasphemy, heresy, and sacrilege have never been worse in history. I cannot conceive how it could ever be any worse than what I just recorded.

To this day, Liew still possesses a theological degree. How it has not been revoked yet, and how he has not been terminated and excommunicated from the school and church, is unfathomable. At this point, they'd be better off giving an unbeliever his job. They'd probably have more respect for the Holy Bible than he does! God forgive him for all the imbecilic garbage he has spewed to young impressionable souls during his career. While I believe that Liew takes the cake for some of the most blasphemous things that I've ever heard, there is actually a world leader who comes very close. The President of the Philippines has publicly called God "stupid."

In a 2018 Davao speech, President Rodrigo Duterte spoke on the Creation account from our Bible. He talked about Adam and Eve eating the forbidden fruit, and about the concept of original sin. "Adam ate it, and malice was born... Who is this *stupid* God? He's a stupid son of a b*tch if that's the case. Creating something perfect, and then thinking of an event to tempt and to destroy the quality of your work." Sadly, it is not the first time that he spoke so unbelievably disrespectful about our Creator. He has called the doctrine of the Trinity - the Father, Son, and Holy Spirit - "silly." He even used vulgar language to attack our Lord Jesus Christ, and what He did for us on the Cross. He said, "Your God was nailed on the Cross. F**k! How unimpressive."

As I questioned how Liew could still hold his job after such sacrilegious remarks, just how in the world does Duterte remain the chosen leader of an *entire country* after those inconceivable blasphemous words? His statements are beyond the pale. Sadly, he is not the only one in the public eye who regularly mocks and disrespects our God. Hollywood celebrities, like Sarah Silverman, and popular musicians, like Marilyn Manson, are notorious for it. Last chapter, I mentioned Ariana Grande and her blasphemous hit song, *"God is a Woman."* And since most liberals today hate our God's Laws, especially those prohibiting abortion and same-sex relations, many echo Grande's opinion.

At 2018's *Emmy Awards*, the actress Thandie Newton said, "I don't even believe in God, but I'm gonna thank HER tonight." 20 years ago, that comment would have (and should have) destroyed her career. Unfortunately, she received a rousing standing ovation for her blasphemous remarks. Liberals also mock and disparage a specific holy figure of our God, and that happens to be the holiest Woman that ever lived - the Mother of our Lord Jesus, the Virgin Mary. They don't like how she lived her life so chaste, holy, pure, and submissive to the LORD. Feminists seem to hate pretty much everything about her. Meanwhile, God has said that she is blessed above all other women - past, present, and future - and *she should be*. Don't tell the left-wing women that, as they will go bonkers.

During an International Women's Day protest in Argentina, in 2017, feminists staged a mock abortion on a woman portraying Mary. Photos of the disgusting act showed blood and baby parts gushing out from between Mary's legs, as the woman dressed as Mary pumped her fist in the air. She was wearing a rosary around her neck, no less, and laughed throughout the sickening spectacle. This took place in front of a cathedral. Frank Pavone, a pro-life priest, said to LifeSite, "This act shows what is at the foundation of hardcore pro-abortion people. They hate the Church, and they literally want to abort Jesus off the face of the earth." Pavone was spot on, as a placard at the U.S. Women's March read - "If Mary had an abortion, we wouldn't be in this mess."

Another marcher carried a sign depicting Mary as a bloody vagina. She is also disrespected at Christmastime. The God-haters don't want to hear about the miraculous birth of our Saviour, and so they've been trying to push Him out of the global celebration of His birth for years now. Thankfully, they have failed - as we God-fearing Christians do our best every year to remind people Who the Reason for the season truly is, and that Christmas begins with CHRIST. Since the antichrists among us have not succeeded in pushing Him out, many resort to blaspheming Him instead.

Not only are atheists putting up Satanic monuments next to Nativity Scenes, but some have even created their own nativities to mock Him. For instance, a zombie Nativity Scene contains the baby Jesus resembling a creature from a horror film. Others have vandalized Nativities or have stolen the figure of Jesus from them. These people must really hate our God with a passion. One of the most blasphemous protests to Christmas that I've seen is the trend of "Gaytivity" scenes. A few years ago, a comedienne posted an image on Twitter of a Nativity Scene in California featuring two Josephs - with Mary being *removed* altogether. LGBT advocates ate it up, and erected Gaytivity scenes of their own. The Josephs were painted pink, and knelt beside baby Jesus.

Upon sharing her sacrilegious image, Carmen Esposito wrote, "Our neighbors' two Joseph nativity is up and I'm beaming." She was actually celebrating her neighbors making a mockery out of our Lord's birth. Her post had gone viral, and she'd received more than 3,000 retweets and over 20,000 likes. Twitter erupted with others sharing images of Gaytivities, or tweeting their messages of support for the disgraceful decor. Some of the comments that really disgusted me were: "Here come the three wise men. Now it's a party" ... "The Bible says that Jesus had two dads" ... "Jesus, Marty & Joseph." Someone had even shared a lesbian Gaytivity, featuring two Marys.

The "three wise men" comment obviously meant to transform the Bible's most important story into a gay orgy. No words could ever describe the disgust I feel for such repulsive blasphemy. As to the argument that "Jesus had two dads." It may be true, but not in the way that they want it to be. Jesus had His Father in Heaven, Almighty God YHWH. Jesus was also given an earthly father by YHWH, to raise and protect Him when He was a child - Joseph. So, while Jesus did have two Dads, they most certainly were not "romantically involved" like the Twitter user grossly implied. One Father was in Heaven, and one was on the earth. Period. Nothing "homosexual" can ever be construed by that.

As to "Jesus, Marty, and Joseph," people tweeting it must be atheists, because they're slapping God in the Face and spitting on His Word. The depraved souls took the event that began the Love Story between God and man, and perverted it into homosexual filth. They must be convinced that there is no God, because how else could you blaspheme the Saviour of your soul and His Godly parents? As much as the LGBT advocates love to reinterpret the

Bible, in order to justify sinful lifestyles, the fact is that they can never change the truth. When God-haters come to this realization, they stop trying to alter God's Word and attack it instead - either verbally or violently.

One example of such an attack on the Holy Bible (which has sadly become all too common in this generation) involves Kelsey L. Munger, a contributor to dirtrag websites like Huffington Post and Salon. Most of her blogs are attacks on Christianity and the Word of God. Her absolute worst was published on the HuffPost website, and was about "ripping up" her Bible. Now you see why I have such a hatred for the Huffington Post. Of all the writers in the world, with important things to say, this news outlet thinks a blog about desecrating God's Word is great reading material.

Munger wrote, "This is a violent and sacrilegious assault on a holy book - THE Holy Book. It is a declaration of my freedom... Rip rip rip... I never thought I would want to destroy a book, but now I feel as if I won't find peace until the job is done... Rip rip rip..." After a long profane description of her destruction of the Holiest Book on Earth, she said, "Finally, when nothing is left but a pile of paper shreds, I stop. The Bible no longer exists. I have forcefully ripped it out of the present tense and damned it to the past tense. It is gone." How demonic has our society become to allow such unholy filth?! On top of that, to be published on one of the top five news sites on the net? How far our nation has fallen!

Meanwhile, liberals have the gall to ask why the LORD can allow California to be burnt to the ground in historic wildfires, or major U.S. cities to be flooded by the record-breaking hurricanes. Their rebellion is all fun and games until the LORD shows up to rain on their parade. As for examples of violent blasphemous acts against the LORD and His Word, two were carried out just a few months before I published this book. A deranged man broke into a church in Virginia, in November 2018, vandalized it, and then proceeded to tear pages out of the Holy Bible. One month later, security footage captured a vandal urinating on two angel statues before smashing them to the ground outside a New York church. I cannot recall a time in history where God's been so disrespected.

This leads me to believe that the Rapture is nearer than ever before, because it appears the seven-year Tribulation of the Book of Revelation is just around the corner. In the 16th Chapter of the Book, inhabitants of the earth blaspheme God *three times* when vials of His wrath are poured out. This is the ultimate blasphemy; because, in this case, they are blaspheming all three members of the Trinity - Father, Son, and Holy Spirit. Just two decades ago, it was impossible to imagine a majority of this world blaspheming the LORD with one accord. Today, it appears to be much more plausible. Thank God that we believers won't be here when they do. Come Lord Jesus!

MEN BLASPHEMED THE NAME OF GOD, WHICH HATH POWER OVER THESE PLAGUES: AND THEY REPENTED NOT TO GIVE HIM GLORY... AND BLASPHEMED THE GOD OF HEAVEN BECAUSE OF THEIR PAINS AND THEIR SORES, AND REPENTED NOT OF THEIR DEEDS... AND MEN BLASPHEMED GOD BECAUSE OF THE PLAGUE OF THE HAIL.

- REVELATION 16:9, 11 & 21

CHAPTER TWELVE

SIN ABOUNDS AND LOVE WAXES COLD

JESUS SAID, BECAUSE INIQUITY SHALL ABOUND, THE LOVE OF
MANY SHALL WAX COLD.

- MATTHEW 24:12

IN MATTHEW, CHAPTER 24, after Lord Jesus had prophesied
to His disciples many of the signs that I have written about in my
books, He said iniquity (sin) would abound in the season of His
return. The Greek word for "iniquity" also means "lawlessness."
So, not only will the world be drenched in sin, but any respect for
God's Law will be thrown out the window. It will be because of a
lack of Godly morality across the globe why Jesus said "the love
of many shall *wax cold*." These words can mean two things...

One: In the sense of the whole world, He means that people
will become selfish and hate one another; and the love He came to
teach will be hard to find. Two: In the sense of us Christians, He
means (due to widespread departure from God's Laws within the
Church) dissensions will arise and brotherly love will cease to be.

Also, due to all of the other signs that I have written about -
persecution, spiritual deceptions, emerging false religions, God's
Law being at odds with modern-day social norms, lack of Biblical
truth being preached from pulpits, perilous times, false prophets,
and doctrines of demons - many will fall away from the Faith and

lose their love for God. Can we see this prophecy of Lord Jesus coming to pass in either of the ways that I have described above? The answer would unfortunately be *absolutely* - on both counts. As far as the world is concerned, whatever you wanna call it - sin, iniquity, transgression, or lawlessness, evil is blanketing the earth.

So, how exactly have historically-Christian nations fallen so far away from the LORD in these Last Days? As technology has increased, the devil seems to find more and more tools that he can use to pull us away from God's Word. Whether television, radio, smartphones, or the internet, Satan has taken things that could do a great deal of good for the Kingdom of God and used them to destroy faith. I have written about this in the previous chapters, so I shouldn't have to explain how he utilizes these things to pervert minds, defile hearts, and spoil souls. In America, he has inspired Godless people to use these tools to propagandize the population.

Little by little, the servants of Satan have chipped away at America's Judeo-Christian foundation and have succeeded a great deal in turning this generation away from God. My friends, the Benham Brothers, have done some great research on this subject; and describe the devil's agenda to destroy America as happening in three ways:

1. By eliminating traditional (Biblical) values
2. By creating or infiltrating new rules
3. By exterminating Christian influence

The Bros have said, "traditional values have been entrenched for so long in American culture and government that atheist and Communist groups have formed to create systematic strategies to eliminate these values." They refer to a book written in 1958, *The Naked Communist*, as a prime example of anti-Christian strategies that Satan has successfully utilized. The book has long served as a step-by-step guide for all God-hating Americans, teaching them how to erode the moral foundation of our country. Here are some steps laid out in the book -

- Eliminate prayer in the schools on the grounds that it violates the principle of separation of Church and State.

- Discredit the family as an institution, and encourage promiscuity and easy divorce.

- Get control of the schools. Use them as transmission belts for socialism. Soften the curriculum, and get control of teacher associations.

- Eliminate all laws governing obscenity by calling them censorship and a violation of free speech and free press.

- Break down cultural standards of morality by promoting pornography in books, magazines, motion pictures, and television.

- Homosexuality, degeneracy, and promiscuity should be portrayed as normal, natural, and healthy.

- Infiltrate the press. Gain control of key positions in radio, TV, and motion pictures.

- Infiltrate the churches and replace revealed religion with social religion. Discredit the Bible.

Sound like modern America? I want to go down the list and see if the Godless radicals have achieved any of these goals...

Eliminate prayer in schools - check. Discredit the institution of family - check. Encourage promiscuity and divorce - check.

Get control of the schools - check. Eliminate laws that govern obscenity - check. Break down the basic standards of morality by promoting pornography - check. Portray homosexual lifestyles as normal, natural, and healthy - check. Infiltrate the press (just how many times have I written about the Godless mainstream media?) - check. Infiltrate the churches - check. Replace revealed religion with social religion - check. And then, there's the final step - the step that would make all of the other goals achievable - discredit the Holy Bible... check.

To "discredit" something is defined as "harming the good reputation of something." Now, I (and hopefully everyone reading this) could never view God's Word in a negative light - as that is impossible for any true believer to do. But there are sadly many Americans who've been deceived and programmed to do so. The Biblically-hostile media mocks the Word of God on a daily basis, and promotes lies that the Holy Bible is just a bunch of stories and moral laws written for a different time in history. They paint God's Law as archaic, bigoted, discriminatory, and even hateful. So, have they succeeded in discrediting the Holy Bible?

Stand in a crowd of people at your job, a secular venue, or on the street, and say these phrases aloud: "I believe in the One *True* God, the God of the Bible" - "Jesus Christ is the *only way*" - "God *created* the Universe" - "Man was created by the LORD, and *did not evolve*" - "Islam, Buddhism, Hinduism, and all other faiths besides Judaism and Christianity are false and *of the devil*" - "Abortion is *murder*" - "There are only *two genders:* Male and Female" - "I *oppose* Gay Marriage." Would you feel comfortable saying these things aloud? Most likely not. Why wouldn't you feel comfortable saying these things publicly if you truly believe them? We should boldly state these things whenever - wherever.

The reason some won't is because they know our society has been brainwashed into believing whatever the media tells them to believe; and the powers that be want you to believe *everything but* the Holy Bible. Thus, they've done their best to discredit it. If you believe it, preach it, and stand up for it, then you become *public enemy number one* in today's America. The Benham Bros pointed back to a Guide Magazine from 1987, titled *"The Overhauling of Straight America."* The article laid out a series of steps for gay activists, like the *Naked Communist* had done, that would lead to normalization of homosexuality in America. It would also lead to demonization of Holy Bible believers, and anyone who opposed the "Gay Rights" movement. The Final Step read:

"At a later stage in our campaign for rights, it will be time to get tough with the remaining opponents. To be blunt, *they must be vilified*. We intend to make those opposed to us look *so nasty* that the average Americans will want to disassociate themselves from *such types*."

Welcome to 2019 America. They've done exactly what they said they would. "By any means necessary" is the battle cry of all Americans who've opposed Christianity and the Holy Bible, and that's how we have gotten to where we are today. Sin abounds all around us. It's been allowed to fester unchecked by much of the Church for decades. Thus, love has grown cold in our country and hate is widespread. Either us Christians are being hated by this "anything goes" society, or some Americans are hating everyone who is not of the same political persuasion. I believe that is where love for our neighbors has waxed coldest in this nation today: in the world of politics.

Obviously, if you've read my previous book, you can derive that I don't vote for Democrats. I don't vote for every Republican either, but I do side with them a lot more because they stand for my Biblical values far more than the Dems do. I don't believe that either party can *save* the nation, because only Jesus can do that. I don't think either will *make America great again*, because only

God can do that. Unfortunately, some Christians today become so entrenched on their political side of the aisle that they don't even view the other side as human beings - hating political adversaries with a passion. I can never recall a time, throughout my life, in which the political climate of our country was so polarized.

While the left-wing liberals oppose just about everything that I stand for, I still do not hate them. Like I said in my previous book, I hate Islam and LGBT Pride, but I don't hate the Muslim people or homosexuals. You can hate an idea, but don't ever hate the people behind the idea. You can dislike what they stand for, but don't ever wish evil upon them. If they wrong you, then leave vengeance to the LORD. It is possible to love someone that you disagree with. Our Lord Jesus had commanded us to "love your enemies" and to "do good to those" who persecute us.

That is what separates believers from the rest of humanity. No other faith teaches such things. Our calling is to lead others to the Lord. How can we ever do that if we are constantly shouting or cursing at those with whom we disagree? We can't. We should calmly debate adversaries and preach truth to them. If they want to shout us down, then let them. We must behave like Jesus. No matter how much we are persecuted for our beliefs in this world, we must never become so bitter that we allow hate to enter our hearts. Hate is a product of the devil. God is love. And we must always represent our loving God to this unbelieving world, and never stoop to their level.

When Jesus was hung on the Cross, He *prayed for* those who put Him there. He asked His Father in Heaven to forgive them. Our God has the right to hate every one of us every day, because we are all covered in sin - and He *hates* sin. Yet, He loves us even though He hates what we do. That is what we are called to do - love our neighbors, even though we may hate what they do. God loved us poor sinners so much that He sent His Son to die for us, so that we could be reconciled unto Him. Now, He expects us to love like He does. You can hate what someone stands for all day long; but as for the person, you need to love them. Period.

On my website, and in my books, I've constantly criticized men and women - by name - for abominable things that they have done. Whether those people are Presidents, Popes, popular actors, musicians, false prophets, or atheists, I've always rebuked anyone if they say or do anything against God. Yet, I pray for them - that the LORD would open their eyes to understand Him. I criticize, I rebuke, and then I *pray* for my enemies - but I *never* hate them. I know this may sound difficult to do in our highly charged political climate, as we're more divided than any other time since the Civil War, but we can never allow our contentions to turn into hate. As Christians, there are 3 steps to follow concerning our enemies -

1. **PRAY** for your enemies. Do not prey on them.

2. **BLESS** them, and do not curse them.

3. **DO GOOD** to them, even if they do nothing but evil to you. For we cannot overcome evil *with* evil, we can only overcome evil with GOOD (Romans 12:14-21).

In our generation, the Matthew 24:12 prophecy of Lord Jesus is being fulfilled in the Christian community just as much as it has been in the world. Lawlessness abounds in the Church today more so than ever before in history since the Dark Ages. Popular Megachurches are refusing to preach on sin, priests molest kids, pastors are sexually abusing vulnerable young women, preachers are using God's tithes to enrich their own lavish lifestyles while their flocks starve, and some churches even celebrate sin, such as abortion and LGBT Pride. Because of all this, as with the world, the love of many Christians has waxed cold.

There are some who refuse to even enter a church because of a scarring experience in their past. Others depart from the Faith altogether because of abuse from wolves in sheep's clothing, who posed as men of God. There are also those who develop a hatred for God, Himself, because of sinful things that were done to them or that they'd seen done in "the Church." The Lutherans disagree with Evangelicals, or Baptists spar with Catholics, and so on and so forth. There are billions of Christians globally and yet so much dissension. The devil loves to divide us. In the earliest days of our Faith, all believers were one in Christ. In the days of the apostles, due to doctrinal disputes, the Church was divided into two sects; but brotherly love still continued despite the disagreements.

Flash-forward to today, and there are dozens - if not hundreds - and some say thousands - of Christian denominations. What we are seeing is not just a minor doctrinal dispute here and there, but many so-called believers are thinking that they know better than everyone else - and that *their* way is the *only way* to know God. There are too many arguments about baptism, Sabbath-keeping, healing, tithing, grace, prophecy, pre-Trib or post-Trib Rapture, is the Holy Bible literal or allegorical, etc.

It is healthy to have disputes, especially within the Church; because the truth is revealed when wise and learned men of God, who are filled with the Spirit, come together and reason with one another. What is *not* healthy is when believers get puffed up in their own pride, shouting down other believers who dare disagree with their opinion on the Word. We see too much of this today. It is a shame. While it is nothing new for believers to disagree, what is new (and extremely sad) is how much so-called Christians can flat-out hate each other. My brothers and sisters, this should not be so! We must realize what the first two Christian denominations had realized - that we have one very important thing that unites us all… our Lord and Saviour, JESUS CHRIST.

I personally don't care if you are Adventist, Baptist, Catholic, Evangelical, Lutheran, or belong to any other denomination under the sun; as long as you believe that Christ was born of a Virgin, died on the Cross for our sins, rose from the dead, and is coming back down to Earth again, then YOU are my brother and sister. It is that simple. While the love of the world may be waxing cold, it should not be so amongst believers; because our King is coming! It is about time that we live - *and LOVE* - like He is.

HE WHICH TESTIFIETH THESE THINGS SAITH, SURELY I COME QUICKLY. AMEN. EVEN SO, COME, LORD JESUS.

- REVELATION 22:20

ACKNOWLEDGMENTS

TO GOD - THANK YOU for mercifully pulling me out of my old sinful life and into service to You. If someone would have told me 20 years ago that I would be studying Your Holy Word every day, and preaching repentance to sinners, I would have said they were crazy. Yet, You knew from my Mother's womb what You willed for me to be and were beyond patient in waiting for me to finally come around.

I'm so grateful to know You LORD, through Your Son, and I pray that You will continue to draw closer to me each and every new day. Words cannot express just how humbled I am that You allow me to serve You. Thank You for being such a Good Father. Thank You for every gift and blessing that You've ever bestowed upon me. Thank You especially for Jesus and Your Spirit. I love You forever YHWH.

To Christ Jesus - I wrote in the dedication how thankful I am to You, and for You, and there will never be enough human words to ever fully describe how much I love You Lord. Glory to You.

To the Holy Spirit - YOU are the Author of my books. I am simply the vessel that You have used to put Your thoughts onto paper. I in no way claim that every word I've written in my books comes directly from You, as I am an imperfect human being who is prone to mistakes; but I do attribute any of my words that lead to the salvation of souls all to You. I have done my best to convey all that You have placed on my heart, and I pray that You will continue to guide me and perfect my craft to glorify You, Lord Jesus, and the Father in Heaven, always.

To Mom, Dad, Bro, Jacob, and Family - I love you all more than you will ever know. I thank God for every one of you daily, and pray the LORD blesses and keeps you all healthy and well all the days that we share on Earth. May God be with you all forever.

To Jason and David Benham - I can never thank you guys enough for all that you've done for me and my website over the years. You've taken time out every year for the annual Christmas Special, and I am honoured to share your articles. As busy as the two of you are, you still take time to respond quickly whenever I reach out to you about anything. I don't believe that there could ever be two men of God in this world that I could ever admire more. God bless you and your families always. Love ya' Bros!

To all those who have supported my website and books - I hope that your faith has been strengthened by my words. Thank you for the interest that you have shown, as it encourages me to do more study, research, and writing each new day. These books would not have been possible without the support of every one of you. As long as you continue to enjoy them, I'll continue to write them as the Spirit guides me to do so.

NOTES

CHAPTER ONE: THE SIGNS OF OUR TIMES CONTINUE

1. "END ANTI-SEMITISM: I'm A Christian - Therefore, I Love the Jews," BiblicalSigns.com, October 30, 2018, https://biblicalsignsintheheadlines.com/2018/10/30/end-anti-semitism-im-a-christian-therefore-i-love-the-jews/

2. "MODERATE ISLAM?: Linda Sarsour Calls For Jihad in America, Tells Fellow Muslims Not to Assimilate," BiblicalSigns.com, July 6, 2017, https://biblicalsignsintheheadlines.com/2017/07/06/moderate-islam-linda-sarsour-calls-for-jihad-in-america-tells-fellow-muslims-to-not-assimilate/

3. "WAR ON CHRISTIANITY: Liberals Are Relentless in Their Attacks on Holy Bible Believers," BiblicalSigns.com, August 17, 2018, https://biblicalsignsintheheadlines.com/2018/08/17/war-on-christianity-liberals-are-relentless-in-their-attacks-on-holy-bible-believers/

4. "ISRAEL VS. HAMAS: Everything That You Need to Know About Their Clashes in 2018," BiblicalSigns.com, July 25, 2018, https://biblicalsignsintheheadlines.com/2018/07/25/israel-vs-hamas-everything-that-you-need-to-know-about-their-clashes-in-2018/

5. "ANOTHER RARE SIGN IN THE HEAVENS: Longest Blood Moon of the Century Rises Tonight," BiblicalSigns.com, July 27, 2018, https://biblicalsignsintheheadlines.com/2018/07/27/another-rare-sign-in-the-heavens-longest-blood-moon-of-the-century-rises-tonight/

6. "THE FORERUNNER?: Alaska's 7.0 Magnitude Earthquake Could Be First of Many Powerful Quakes to Rattle USA," BiblicalSigns.com, November 30, 2018, https://biblicalsignsintheheadlines.com/2018/11/30/the-forerunne r-alaskas-7-0-magnitude-earthquake-could-be-first-of-many-pow erful-quakes-to-rattle-usa/

7. "HURRICANE MICHAEL: The Storm I Have Long Warned About Has Arrived, And It Is Making History," BiblicalSigns.com, October 10, 2018, https://biblicalsignsintheheadlines.com/2018/10/10/hurricane-mic hael-the-storm-that-i-warned-of-has-arrived-and-it-is-making-hi story/

CHAPTER TWO: MORE SIGNS CONTINUE

1. "CONFORM OR ELSE: Transgender Activists Threatening Those Who Refuse To Embrace Their Radical Ideology," BiblicalSigns.com, December 7, 2018, https://biblicalsignsintheheadlines.com/2018/12/07/conform-or-el se-transgender-activists-threatening-those-who-refuse-to-embrac e-their-radical-ideology/

2. "THE SAD 'STATE OF THEOLOGY': New Survey Reveals Americans (Even Some Christians) Are Biblically-Illiterate," BiblicalSigns.com, October 19, 2018, https://biblicalsignsintheheadlines.com/2018/10/19/the-sad-state- of-theology-new-survey-reveals-americans-even-some-christians- are-biblically-illiterate/

CHAPTER THREE: MASS SHOOTINGS

1. "AMERICA DOESN'T NEED GUN CONTROL - AMERICA DOESN'T NEED MORE GUNS - AMERICA NEEDS JESUS," BiblicalSigns.com, May 18, 2018, https://biblicalsignsintheheadlines.com/2018/05/18/america-does nt-need-gun-control-america-doesnt-need-more-guns-america-ne eds-jesus/

2. "YOU CANNOT BE "PRO-LIFE" AND A MURDERER, IT IS AN OXYMORON," BiblicalSigns.com, December 1, 2015, https://biblicalsignsintheheadlines.com/2015/12/01/you-cannot-be-pro-life-and-a-murderer-it-is-an-oxymoron/

3. "DEADLIEST SHOOTING IN U.S. HISTORY: Islamic Terrorist Massacres Gays," BiblicalSigns.com, June 12, 2016, https://biblicalsignsintheheadlines.com/2016/06/12/deadliest-mass-shooting-in-u-s-history-muslim-terrorist-massacres-gays/

4. "OF THE DEVIL: 'Irreligious' Terrorist Carries Out Deadliest Mass Shooting in U.S. History," BiblicalSigns.com, October 2, 2017, https://biblicalsignsintheheadlines.com/2017/10/02/of-the-devil-irreligious-terrorist-carries-out-deadliest-mass-shooting-in-u-s-history/

CHAPTER FOUR: RACISM

1. "RACISM: What Does God Have to Say About It?," BiblicalSigns.com, October 19, 2017, https://biblicalsignsintheheadlines.com/2017/10/19/racism-what-does-god-have-to-say-about-it/

2. "A NATION DIVIDED: 'No Justice, No Peace' Must Become 'Know Jesus, Know Peace'," BiblicalSigns.com, July 9, 2016, https://biblicalsignsintheheadlines.com/2016/07/09/a-nation-divided-no-justice-no-peace-must-become-know-jesus-know-peace/

CHAPTER FIVE: HISTORIC WILDFIRES

1. "JUDGMENT BY FIRE: 'Apocalyptic Scenes' in California As Wildfires Rage," BiblicalSigns.com, October 11, 2017, https://biblicalsignsintheheadlines.com/2017/10/11/judgment-by-fire-apocalyptic-scenes-in-california-as-wildfires-rage/

2. "HOLY FIRE: 'Largest Wildfire in California History' May Be Long-Overdue Judgment Upon Godless State," BiblicalSigns.com, August 6, 2018, https://biblicalsignsintheheadlines.com/2018/08/06/holy-fire-apocalyptic-wildfires-may-be-long-overdue-judgment-of-god-upon-godless-california/

3. "HELL ON EARTH: 'Paradise Destroyed' in California As Wildfires Once Again Rage Across Godless State," BiblicalSigns.com, November 9, 2018, https://biblicalsignsintheheadlines.com/2018/11/09/hell-on-earth-paradise-destroyed-in-california-as-wildfires-once-again-rage-across-godless-state/

CHAPTER SIX: PESTILENCES

1. "THERE WILL BE PESTILENCES: Greater Risk of Global Pandemic Than Ever Before," BiblicalSigns.com, April 4, 2017, https://biblicalsignsintheheadlines.com/2017/04/04/there-will-be-pestilences-greater-risk-of-global-pandemic-than-ever-before/

CHAPTER SEVEN: WARS AND RUMOURS OF WARS

1. "RUMOURS OF WARS: Biblical Battles on the Horizon," BiblicalSigns.com, April 7, 2017, https://biblicalsignsintheheadlines.com/2017/04/07/rumours-of-wars-biblical-battles-on-the-horizon/
2. "ALLIED AGAINST ISRAEL: Is the Gog-Magog War At the Door?," BiblicalSigns.com, February 14, 2018, https://biblicalsignsintheheadlines.com/2018/02/14/allied-against-israel-is-the-gog-magog-war-at-the-door/
3. "NUCLEAR TSUNAMI: Russian Bombs Detonated on Sea Floor Could Drown Major U.S. Cities," BiblicalSigns.com, May 2, 2017, https://biblicalsignsintheheadlines.com/2017/05/02/nuclear-tsunami-russian-bombs-on-sea-floor-could-drown-major-u-s-cities/
4. "NUCLEAR NORTH KOREA: The Threat Is Real," BiblicalSigns.com, July 30, 2017, https://biblicalsignsintheheadlines.com/2017/07/30/nuclear-north-korea-the-threat-is-real/
5. "EXISTENTIAL THREAT: Enemies of America Plot EMP Attacks," BiblicalSigns.com, April 25, 2016, https://biblicalsignsintheheadlines.com/2016/04/25/existential-threat-enemies-of-america-plot-emp-attacks/

Chapter Eight: "2nd Timothy 3" Generation

1. "I STAND AGAINST PRIDE: Christians Cannot Stand With God AND the LGBT Movement (So Pick A Side)," BiblicalSigns.com, June 10, 2017, https://biblicalsignsintheheadlines.com/2017/06/10/i-stand-agains t-pride-christians-cannot-stand-with-god-and-the-lgbt-movemen t-so-pick-a-side/

2. "KAVANAUGH CONTROVERSY: Dems Aren't About Protecting Women - Only About Preserving A Liberal SCOTUS," BiblicalSigns.com, September 24, 2018, https://biblicalsignsintheheadlines.com/2018/09/24/kavanaugh-co ntroversy-dems-arent-about-protecting-women-only-about-prese rving-a-liberal-scotus/

3. "CONFIRM KAVANAUGH NOW: The Christian Case For Why He Should Be Sitting On the Supreme Court," BiblicalSigns.com, October 5, 2018, https://biblicalsignsintheheadlines.com/2018/10/05/confirm-kava naugh-now-the-christian-case-for-why-he-should-be-sitting-on-t he-supreme-court/

4. "WAR ON CHRISTIANITY: Liberals Are Relentless In Their Attacks On Holy Bible Believers," BiblicalSigns.com, August 17, 2018, https://biblicalsignsintheheadlines.com/2018/08/17/war-on-christ ianity-liberals-are-relentless-in-their-attacks-on-holy-bible-believ ers/

Chapter Nine: False Prophets

1. "SIN: The Word Nobody Wants To Hear, But Should," BiblicalSigns.com, November 10, 2015, https://biblicalsignsintheheadlines.com/2015/11/10/society-of-sin-why-stopping-it-starts-with-us/

2. "THE POPE'S LOVE AFFAIR WITH ISLAM: Is Francis Revelation's 'False Prophet'?," BiblicalSigns.com, August 1, 2016, https://biblicalsignsintheheadlines.com/2016/08/01/the-popes-lov e-affair-with-islam-is-francis-revelations-false-prophet/

3. "FALSE PROPHET: Megachurch Pastor Tells Christians To 'Forget' the Ten Commandments," BiblicalSigns.com, January 10, 2019, https://biblicalsignsintheheadlines.com/2019/01/10/false-prophet-megachurch-pastor-tells-christians-to-forget-the-ten-commandments/

Chapter Ten: Demonic Indoctrination

1. "DEMONIC INDOCTRINATION: The Devil In Your TV," BiblicalSigns.com, February 9, 2016, https://biblicalsignsintheheadlines.com/2016/02/09/demonic-indoctrination-the-devil-in-your-tv/

2. "TARGETING YOUR KIDS: Disney Joins Forces With Gay Lobby To Push LGBT Agenda On Children," BiblicalSigns.com, March 3, 2017, https://biblicalsignsintheheadlines.com/2017/03/03/targeting-your-kids-disney-joins-forces-with-gay-lobby-to-push-lgbt-agenda-on-children/

3. "SUPPRESSING SPEECH: Exposing Facebook's War On Conservative Christians," BiblicalSigns.com, March 31, 2017, https://biblicalsignsintheheadlines.com/2017/03/31/suppressing-speech-exposing-facebooks-war-on-conservative-christians/

4. "BLATANT OMISSION: Google Home Knows Allah, Muhammad, Buddha, and Satan, But Not Jesus," BiblicalSigns.com, January 26, 2018, https://biblicalsignsintheheadlines.com/2018/01/26/blatant-omission-google-home-knows-allah-muhammad-buddha-and-satan-but-not-jesus/

5. "SATANIC WORSHIP ON THE RISE IN AMERICA," BiblicalSigns.com, November 3, 2015, https://biblicalsignsintheheadlines.com/2015/11/03/satanic-worship-on-the-rise-in-america/

Chapter Eleven: Widespread Blasphemy

1. "BEYOND BLASPHEMY: Gay Co-Founder of 'Queer Theology' Claims Jesus Was a Polyamorous 'Slut'," BiblicalSigns.com, November 19, 2018, https://biblicalsignsintheheadlines.com/2018/11/19/beyond-blasphemy-gay-co-founder-of-queer-theology-claims-jesus-was-a-polyamorous-slut/

2. "VITRIOL AGAINST THE VIRGIN: The Blasphemy of the Radical Left Knows No Bounds," BiblicalSigns.com, March 14, 2017, https://biblicalsignsintheheadlines.com/2017/03/14/vitriol-against-the-virgin-the-blasphemy-of-the-radical-left-knows-no-bounds/

3. "WAR ON THE CHRIST OF CHRISTMAS CONTINUES: God-Haters Blaspheme, Mock, And Pervert the Birth of Jesus," BiblicalSigns.com, December 1, 2017, https://biblicalsignsintheheadlines.com/2017/12/01/war-on-the-christ-of-christmas-continues-god-haters-blaspheme-mock-and-pervert-the-birth-of-jesus/

Chapter Twelve: Sin Abounds and Love Waxes Cold

1. "CHRISTIANS IN THE CROSSHAIRS OF A DARK AGENDA," BenhamBrothers.com, February 16, 2016, https://benhambrothers.com/christians-cross-hairs-dark-agenda/

2. "LOVE YOUR ENEMIES: Threatening Lives of Political Adversaries Is Not the Way of 'the Right'," BiblicalSigns.com, October 26, 2018, https://biblicalsignsintheheadlines.com/2018/10/26/love-your-enemies-threatening-the-lives-of-political-adversaries-is-not-the-way-of-the-right/

ABOUT THE AUTHOR

MICHAEL SAWDY is the Founder of the website *Biblical Signs In The Headlines*, and the Author of *The Signs of Our Times* book series. In 2006, He had a life-changing experience with the Lord Jesus Christ, which led him to turn from a sinful life and to fully dedicate his life to God. Since then, he's spent thousands of hours studying the Bible - along with teachings by some of his greatest influences: the Benham Brothers, Jack Van Impe, Billy Graham, John Hagee, and Chuck Missler.

Due to the message which he received from the Lord, during his salvation experience, MichaEL believes strongly that Jesus is truly coming back soon. This belief is what inspired him to create *BiblicalSigns.com* in 2015, and to write books on "Last Days" Bible Prophecy - specifically concerning the Rapture. His website surpassed over one-million visitors in 2017, and his first book has been a #1 Best Seller in multiple Christian categories on Amazon. Within months of releasing *The Signs of Our Times*, the Spirit had inspired him to write this Sequel.

VISIT THE WEBSITE:
BiblicalSigns.com
FOLLOW ON SOCIAL MEDIA:
Facebook - /BiblicalSignsInTheHeadlines
/TheSignsOfOurTimesBook
Twitter - @MichaelofYHWH (Personal)
@BiblicalSigns (Website)
@SignsOfTimes777 (Books)

Get MichaEL's Best-Selling book - *THE SIGNS OF OUR TIMES: 12 Biblical Reasons Why This Could Be the Generation of the Rapture* - on Amazon, Barnes & Noble, Books-A-Million, Walmart, or at many other online book retailers around the world.

Printed in Great Britain
by Amazon

47869563R00088